# THE LOVE STORY OF
# PARNELL AND KATHARINE O'SHEA

# The Love Story of Parnell and Katharine O'Shea

Margery Brady

THE MERCIER PRESS

The Mercier Press Limited
4 Bridge Street, Cork
24 Lower Abbey Street, Dublin 1

A CIP catalogue record for this book
is available from the British Library

ISBN 0-85342-980-4

For my loved ones

*Printed in Ireland by Colour Books Ltd.*

# Introduction

... Parnell loved his country
And Parnell loved his lass.
W.B. Yeats

There is no doubt that Charles Stewart Parnell was one of Ireland's finest statesmen, the impressive monument to him on Dublin's main street testifies to this fact and is inscribed with his famous words: 'No man has a right to fix the boundary to the march of a nation ....' Admiring the monument, it is hard to believe that this man was removed from the position as leader of his party and lay in a neglected grave for fifty years. The reason — 'Parnell loved his lass'.

His lass, Katharine, had loved and married Willie O'Shea thirteen years before she met Parnell. It was to promote her husband's political career that she invited Parnell to dinner, and thus started the all-consuming love which is the subject of this book.

Within a few months of their meeting, Parnell and Katharine became lovers and he began to think of her as his wife. Katharine says:

> ... as regards the marriage bond his honest conviction was that there is none where intense mutual attraction — commonly called love — does not exist, or where it ceases to exist. To Parnell's heart and conscience I was no more a wife of Captain O'Shea when he first met me than I was after Captain O'Shea had divorced me, ten years later.

Parnell thought that his private life was very much his own and that, to paraphrase his own saying, 'no man had the right to say to his leader: "Thus far shalt thou go and no further"'.

Of the four and twenty books and as many newspaper reports with which I surrounded myself while searching for the truth of the affair, it was in the newspaper reports of the divorce case that the exact details were given of the where-abouts of Parnell and Katharine during the eleven years of their love life. These provided the bones for this story which was fleshed out with Katharine's own tale and the other fascinating facts given elsewhere.

# Acknowledgements

For assistance in the writing of this book I am most grateful to my editor, Emer Ryan, and to The Mercier Press. Thanks are also due in Kilkenny to Frank McEvoy of Hebron Books; the staff of Kilkenny County Library; Michael O'Dwyer, librarian of Rothe House; Dr Fearghus Farrell, librarian of St. Kieran's College; Brendan Conway, C.E.O. and Seamus Brennan, B.C.L. Invaluable access to old newspapers was given by the staff of Pearse Street Library, Dublin, and by the British Library — the latter researched by my son, Maurice, and Tanya Corrie. Advice on the cause of Parnell's death was sought from Doctors Ailish and Kieran Cuddihy. Prof. P.A. Wayman, Dunsink Observatory provided the gem of information concerning the meteor that fell as Parnell was buried, and Mr L.J. Reilly, Local History Assistant, Greenwich, gave historical details of Eltham and the houses of Katharine and Aunt Ben. The staff of the Brighton Hotel showed me the sitting room of 39 Bedford Square, Brighton, now integrated into their hotel, and some members of Blackheath Golf Club gave me a guided tour of Eltham Lodge (including Katharine's bedroom), where Aunt Ben's presence can still be felt.

My loved ones — extended family and friends — gave me encouragement and to these this book is dedicated.

# 1

'That's Parnell himself that's passed', he said, when the
cheering had subsided. 'Ireland's greatest son. I'd sell me hat,
I'd sell me horse and cab. I'd sell meself, by Jasus, I'd nearly
sell me soul if he beckoned me to do it.'

In *I Knock at the Door*, Sean O'Casey's words give some idea
of the charisma of the man, Charles Stewart Parnell.

The legend continues in the description by his fellow
member of parliament, T.P. O'Connor:

> ... his face was one of the handsomest in the House of
> Commons. The nose was long, straight, well-chiselled; the
> mouth was small and well-carved, but mobile with pride,
> passion and scorn; the voice was clear, sure and penetrating
> and, when he was excited, could be thrilling, so that some-
> times you could imagine that it had a power to control and
> even terrorize the House of Commons; his forehead was
> beautiful — perfectly round, white and lofty. But, after all, in
> looking at him, as in the case of every remarkable man, the
> eyes were the most striking feature. They were the most
> meaning eyes I have ever seen. They were of the hard dark
> sort, which you see in the Red Indian — red-brown, like flint;
> but who can describe their varying lights and impressions?
> Sometimes you thought they never changed, for they certainly
> never revealed anything; at others they seemed to flash and
> burn; and they always had a strange glow in them that arrested
> your attention.

In the spring of 1880, the thirty-three-year-old Parnell returned from a tour of America and Canada where he had
gone to rally support from the Irish Americans for victims of
the threatened famine in the west of Ireland. He had collected $200,000 (conversion to today's values appears in brack-
ets throughout — in this case it would be $12,600,000). In
Montreal, Tim Healy, who had travelled with him, made a
speech and hailed him as 'The Uncrowned King of Ireland'
— a title once given to Daniel O'Connell. A general election

for the House of Commons had prompted his return to Ireland where he faced another gruelling tour canvassing for himself and his party.

Parnell had made a name for himself by joining his fellow MP, J.G. Biggar, in the now famous policy of obstruction. With the simple outvoting of Isaac Butt's attempts to have laws passed in favour of Ireland, Biggar and Parnell had begun to make lengthy speeches and raise many questions, thus preventing the progress of parliamentary business. In one debate on coercion, Biggar spoke for four hours, quoting from books. This policy of obstructing parliamentary procedure brought about a change in the law in regard to time spent on any given topic, and won support for Parnell from all of the Irish parties, assuring him of an easy victory in the election of 1880.

Parnell was nominated in three constituencies — Meath, Mayo and Cork. The story of his Cork nomination is interesting. John Horgan tells that on 31 March 1880 — the final day for nominations, his father, Michael J. Horgan, was handed a paper by a known nationalist politician, nominating Parnell for Cork. It was already signed by two Catholic priests. Horgan asked if Parnell had given his assent and was handed £50 (£3,150) in cash which, it was said, came from Parnell with £200 (£12,600) more to follow. Horgan quickly signed the paper and the news of the nomination was greeted with cheers from the public. Parnell sent a telegram of thanks, in which he announced that he would arrive in Cork on 2 April. On his arrival he asked Horgan who had put his name forward, as he knew nothing about it. Further questioning of the nationalist politician revealed that the money had come from the Tory Party, so that a nationalist candidate might take votes from the Whigs. Healy, Parnell's secretary, asked for the balance of the £250 (£15,750) to fight the election, saying that it would be a sweet victory made possible by Tory money.

Parnell won in all three constituencies but chose to represent Cork. Of the 63 'Home Rulers' elected, 24 were definite Parnellites. On 16 May, some of the newly elected Irish members met to discuss the chairmanship of the parliamentary party. William Shaw had replaced Isaac Butt when the latter died, but it was felt that Parnell would make a better leader. Parnell was not informed of this decision until the following day. All of the Irish MPs were invited to a meeting at the City Hall, but 23 failed to arrive. The O'Gorman Mahon proposed Parnell who defeated Shaw by 5 votes.

Among those who voted for Parnell was a man no one seemed to know except The O'Gorman Mahon who had been his running companion for Clare. Once again, we have T.P. O'Connor to thank for his description of this hitherto unknown man:

> ... slightly overdressed, laughing, with the indescribable air of the man whom life had made somewhat cynical, he was in sharp contrast with the rugged, plainly dressed, serious figures round him.

Parnell's first reaction was that this 'dandy' was not the type of candidate the party needed. The newcomer was Captain William Henry O'Shea.

Willie O'Shea was a gambling man. Although he had telegraphed his wife, Katharine, that Parnell might be too 'advanced', he sensed that he would be a winner and had voted for him. Willie's political career was only beginning and his vote for Parnell could prove helpful. He asked Katharine to give dinner parties for politicians who might be useful to him and to include Parnell in her invitations. The dinners were to be held in Thomas's Hotel, Berkeley Square, London. Although Parnell was asked each time, accepting on occasions, declining at other times, he never came.

Unaware that Parnell did not think much of Willie as a party member, Katharine excused his absence, partly because The O'Gorman Mahon had said that the American tour had exhausted Parnell — indeed that he might not 'last out the season' — and partly because stories abounded that he was aloof and did not accept political invitations. Nevertheless, he had seemed sociable enough in Paris and America and some of Katharine's guests laughingly taunted her about the vacant chair, causing her to vow that 'the uncrowned King of Ireland shall sit in that chair at the next dinner I give!'

Katharine loved a challenge and enlisted the help of her sister, Anna, who lived at Buckingham Gate, near the House of Commons. On a sunny summer day, the sisters sent in a card requesting Parnell to meet them in the Palace Yard. Katharine wrote of their first encounter:

> He came out, a tall gaunt figure, thin and deadly pale. He looked straight at me smiling, and his curiously burning eyes looked into mine with a wondering intentness that threw into my brain the sudden thought; 'This man is wonderful — and different.'

They exchanged pleasantries and Katharine asked, since he had not answered her last invitation, if he could be persuaded to come to dinner. Politely, he said that he had not opened his recent post but would be glad to accept on his return from Paris where he would be attending the wedding of his youngest sister, Theodosia, to Commander Claude Paget. Katharine's story continues:

> In leaning forward in the cab to say good-bye a rose I was wearing in my bodice fell out and on to my skirt. He picked it up and, touching it lightly to his lips, placed it in his buttonhole. This rose I found long years afterwards done up in an envelope, with my name and the date, among his most private papers, and when he died I laid it upon his heart.

Katharine was five months older than he, had been married for thirteen years and had three children. The attraction, however, was mutual and immediate. Many versions of this case of love at first sight have been given, including that of

St. John Ervine who described Katharine thus:

> Her face was big and broad and strong, despite her look of emotionalism, and her eyes were large and fine and honest. She had an unusually big, uneven nose which marred her beauty, and her mouth was long and loose and nervous. Had one not known she was English, one might have thought, judging by her portraits, that she was Italian ... She was a resolute woman, not easily diverted from her determinations, and it is likely that her tenacity and decision made her irresistible to Parnell, who, though himself a man of resolution, was, at the time he met her, a sick man suffering from physical exhaustion. She was a robust woman, physically stronger that Parnell, to whom her bodily strength must have been an additional attraction, as it was also a danger.

On 17 July, a few days after their first meeting, Parnell wrote:

> My dear Mrs. O'Shea,

> We have all been in such a 'disturbed' condition that I have been quite unable to wander further from here than a radius of about one hundred paces allons. And this notwithstanding the powerful attractions which have been tending to seduce me from my duty towards my country in the direction of Thomas's Hotel. I am going over to Paris on Monday evening or Tuesday morning to attend my sister's wedding, and on my return, will write you again and ask for an opportunity of seeing you.

It was signed: 'Yours very truly, Chas. S. Parnell'.

Katharine allowed him to select his own date for dining with them and booked a box at the Gaiety Theatre for later in the evening. It was a small dinner party with her sister, Anna Steele, her nephew, Matthew Wood, Justin McCarthy, MP, and a few others. Neither Anna's nor Katharine's husband was present — Anna's because she was separated. Parnell arrived late but apologetic. Political matters did not dominate the conversation and he gave most of his attention to Anna Steele.

At the theatre, Katharine and Parnell gravitated to the dark corner at the back of the box. She was an excellent listener and the usually reticent party leader found himself confiding in her about his love for an American girl.

Eight years previously, while he and his brother, John, had been visiting their uncle's apartment on the Champs Elysées he had met a beautiful blonde American, Miss Woods. The two had been instantly attracted and he had wooed her in Paris and in Rome. His uncle warned him that he might catch the Roman fever and, as he had a morbid fear of death, he hastily left for Avondale, his home in Ireland. All seemed well when he rejoined Miss Woods in Paris, and in the spring of 1871 he returned to Avondale, hoping that she would follow. Suddenly she left for America, and, although he followed her to Newport, the affair faded out. On his recent tour he had called again on this old love but their feelings had not stood the test of time. She had quoted a poem by Elizabeth Barrett Browning:

> Unless you can muse in a crowd all day,
> On the absent face that fixed you,
> Unless you can dream that his faith is fast
> Through behoving and unbehoving,
> Unless you can die when the dream is past
> Oh, never call it loving.

He would not live up to these high demands made by his American love. She quickly returned to her life without him and found consolation elsewhere. Parnell's work for Ireland had finally driven her from his heart.

# 2

The first member of the Parnell family to come to Ireland was Thomas Parnell, son of a gilder and painter. Thomas' grandfather and uncle had both been mayors of Congleton in Cheshire. The family were from merchant stock and when, in the seventeenth century, Thomas decided to emigrate, he could afford to buy an estate in Queen's County (Laois).

His elder son, also Thomas, was born in 1679 and graduated from Trinity College, Dublin, while he was still in his teens. His friends there included Swift, Congreve and Pope, and Thomas Parnell made a name for himself as a minor poet. In 1703, he was ordained, and two years later he was appointed Archbishop of Clogher. He was devoted to his wife, Anne Minchin, of Tipperary and was heartbroken when she and their two sons died young. At this time, aggravated no doubt by his sorrow, he showed signs of manic depression — an illness that was to resurface in the Parnell family in later generations. He died suddenly in 1717, just six years after his wife.

The Queen's County estate passed to his brother, John, a barrister, subsequently a judge, who was a member of the Irish House of Commons. John died ten years later in 1727 and the property passed to his son, also John, who was created a baronet and married Ann Ward of Castle Ward, Co. Down, daughter of a judge.

Their son, the second Sir John, was born on Christmas Day 1744. He and his wife, Letitia Charlotte Brooke, of Fermanagh, had five sons and a daughter. He became Chancellor of the Exchequer and Privy Councillor and also commanded a corps of the Irish Volunteers. He acquired land in Collure, Co. Armagh, on a long lease from Trinity College. In 1795, he also inherited the Avondale estate from a relative, Samuel Hayes. In 1799, he was dismissed from his government office as he would not support the Union. He died two years later.

Their eldest son, John, was deaf and dumb. Henry, the second son, was created Baron Congleton, was active in politics, but eventually became deranged and hanged himself at the age of sixty-six. The third son, William, was grandfather of Charles Stewart Parnell.

William Parnell inherited Avondale and was the first member of the family to live there. A square house, built in 1779 by Samuel Hayes, a notable amateur architect, it had fine James Wyatt plaster work which incorporated mirrors in the drawing-room décor. With it came 4,500 acres of good land, and William enjoyed his life as a country gentleman. Amongst those entertained by William and his wife, Frances Howard, was Thomas Moore, and it was on a visit to Avondale that Moore wrote 'The Meeting of the Waters' about the nearby Vale of Avoca.

When William died in 1821, he left an eight-year-old son, John, and a daughter, Catherine. In 1834, John and his maternal cousin, Lord Powerscourt, set sail for America. In Washington, they met seventeen-year-old Delia Tudor Stewart — a dark-haired, blue-eyed, oval-faced heiress — who captivated the hearts of both men. A version of the story given by their son, John, said that Catherine signed over her share of Avondale for £10,000 (£630,000) with interest of 5 per cent and that this swayed Delia in favour of John, while others say that the sum was an endowment from his father, William. Whichever story is true, Delia apparently loved John more than his cousin, for she married him on 31 May 1834.

Delia Tudor Stewart had a colourful background. Her grandfather, Charles Stewart, and his wife, Sarah Ford, had emigrated from Belfast. Their youngest son of eight children, also Charles, was born in 1778. His father died when he was only two years old and his mother married again. At the age of thirteen, the young Charles ran away to sea and, in time, became a Commodore in the American Navy, and a national hero. When he retired, Lincoln conferred on him the title of Rear Admiral. His wife, Delia Tudor, came from a well-known family. The pair had two children. Their son, Charles the third, made a fortune in timber and railroads, which he later left to his sister, Delia — the bride of 1834.

Delia came back to Avondale with her new husband, John Henry Parnell, but found the life there very dull. Although all of their twelve children were born in Ireland, she returned regularly to America. One child was stillborn and the eldest, William, died at the age of five. The next son, Hayes, was killed in a hunting accident in his sixteenth year, so the brother closest in age to Charles was John Howard, who was three years old when Charles was born on 27 June 1846.

The children were left in the charge of nurses and it was from an English woman, 'Mrs Tupn'y', that John Howard and Charles got their great love of Wicklow. The girls were educated at home by governesses, sent to finishing school in Paris, and launched into society by their uncle, Sir Ralph Howard. There was no school near Avondale for the boys. As Charles was thought to be unruly, his father took him, at the tender age of six, over to a girls' school in Yeovil, Somerset but a dose of typhoid fever brought about an early return. Two years later he was sent to Kirk Langley in Derbyshire and remained longer in this establishment. From 1856 to 1861 he attended the Great Ealing School, London where his brother was also a pupil, but while John was liked his comrades found Charles arrogant and aggressive. While Charles was at this school his father decided to extend his property. In 1858 he bought Clonmore estate in Carlow from his uncle, Sir Ralph Howard, for nearly £70,000 (£4,410,000). This outlay together with the settlement on his sister, Catherine, was a heavy financial burden.

John Parnell had a great liking for cricket and, the year following the purchase of Clonmore, he insisted on playing a match, although suffering from a high temperature. This act of folly brought on a fever which resulted in his untimely death. All the family was in Paris at the time, except for the thirteen-year-old Charles, who had to endure alone the trauma of his father's death and burial in Mount Jerome cemetery. The ordeal had a shattering effect on the boy, who became quite nervous, took to sleepwalking, and developed a horror of death and funerals which was to last a lifetime.

On their return from Paris, Delia and the family went into lodgings near Gardiner Street, Dublin, where John Henry's will was read. He had made no provision for his wife, possibly because she had money of her own. John Howard was given the Collure estate in Armagh, but he had to pay £1,000 (£63,000) rent a year to Trinity along with annuities to his sisters, which left him with little or no money. (Sir Ralph Howard had promised that he would make John Howard his heir but left him only shares in a Welsh mine which proved worthless.) Charles inherited Avondale — which was in considerable debt also — and Henry Tudor was left the Carlow estate.

The children were made wards of Chancery, Avondale was temporarily rented and the Parnell family moved first to a house called Khyber Pass in Dalkey, Co. Dublin, then to Kingstown (Dún Laoghaire) and, after a year, to 14 Upper Temple Street, Dublin.

Charles said that he would like to go to Cambridge and it was thought best to send him first to a cramming school at Chipping Norton in Oxfordshire. This proved effective and he was admitted to Magdalene College, Cambridge, where Mathematics was his principal subject. His three and a half years there were not very productive and came to a shameful end. On 1 May 1869, he and three friends went to the local station for refreshments — champagne, sherry and biscuits — and when they emerged at 10 o'clock one member of the party went to get a cab while Charles 'rested' in the gutter. A manure dealer, Edward Hamilton, came on the scene and offered help which was declined. Some name-calling resulted in a fight and Charles knocked Hamilton to the ground and hit him. The matter ended up in a police station, where Charles was prosecuted and Hamilton was awarded 20 guineas (1,260 guineas) damages. When news of this reached the college authorities, Charles was rusticated for the remainder of the term — a mere fortnight. He went home to his beloved estate at Avondale, and, finding it very neglected, decided not to return to Cambridge but to look after his inheritance.

While he was at Cambridge, his younger sister, Fanny, had contributed verses to a suppressed nationalist newspaper, the *Irish People*. Whether because of Fanny's patriotism or because of her mother's openly acknowledged anti-British feelings, the Parnell house in Temple Street was searched by the police. Nothing incriminating was found but a uniform and sword, worn by Charles when he became a member of the Wicklow militia, were taken away. This mildly annoyed him. However, another event had far greater effect on his politics.

In September 1867, two Fenian members were arrested in Manchester. A group tried to free them from a prison van. Shots were fired to remove the lock and, inadvertently, a policeman inside the door was killed. The three rescuers, Allen, Larkin and O'Brien, were hanged. This sentence was passionately condemned in Ireland, where the three became known as the Manchester Martyrs. A popular ballad enshrined their memory and the tidal wave of patriotism also swept Charles along.

Over the next five years, he settled in to life at Avondale. He took a passing interest in Irish affairs but surprised everyone in 1874 by saying that he was considering running for Parliament. This he could not do until his resignation as High Sheriff for Co. Wicklow was validated. He convinced John to stand instead, then drew up his first political document on his brother's behalf:

To the Electors of the County Wicklow.

Gentlemen,

Believing that the time has arrived for all true Irishmen to unite in the spontaneous demand for justice from England that is now convulsing the country, I have determined to offer myself for the honour of representing you in Parliament.

The principles for which my ancestor, Sir John Parnell, then Chancellor of the Irish Exchequer, refused the peerage from an English Government are still mine, and the cause of the Repeal of the Union under its new name of Home Rule will always find in me a firm and honest supporter.

My experience of the working of the Ulster system of Land Tenure in the North convinces me that there is no other remedy for the unfortunate relations existing between landlord and tenant in the other parts of Ireland than the legalisation through the whole of the country of the Ulster Tenant Right, which is partially Fixture of Tenure, or some equivalent or extension of a custom which has so increased the prosperity of the thriving North.

A residence of several years in America, where Religious and Secular Education are combined, has assured me that the attempt to deprive the youth of the country of spiritual instruction must be put down, and I shall give my support to the Denominational System in connection both with the University and the Primary branches.

Owing to the great tranquillity of the Country, I think it would now be a graceful act to extend the Clemency of the Crown to the remaining Political Prisoners.

My grandfather and uncle represented this County for many years, and as you have experienced their trustworthiness, so I also hope you will believe in mine.

I am, gentlemen,

Yours truly,

John Howard Parnell.

John did not win the seat but when a vacancy arose a few weeks later, Charles himself stood. Making a speech at a meeting in the Rotunda, Dublin, on 9 March 1874, he was visibly nervous, stammered and could not be heard. His nails bit into the palms of his hands. The audience clapped out of sympathy, but many said that he would not be heard of again. He had no more success than his brother, receiving only 1,235 votes, while Colonel Taylor, his opponent, nearly doubled this figure with 2,183.

It was not until 1875 that Charles had his first success on the political stage. This time his candidature was endorsed by the Home Rule League, and he received great acclaim for a speech, finishing with the words:

> England should remember the example set by her American colonies and bear in mind that, if she refuse to Ireland what her people demand as a right, the day would come when Ireland would have her opportunity in England's weakness.

On 22 April, Charles Stewart Parnell took his seat in the House of Commons. On that same day, the Belfast member, Joseph Gillis Biggar, a pork butcher by trade, tried out his new policy of delaying proceedings in the House.

Charles' maiden speech though unimpressive, concluded that Ireland was not a geographical fragment of England, but a nation in its own right. It would be some years before the young Charles would mature into the fine speaker whose reputation rested on his oratory.

During his political career, he was known as 'Parnell' and as such continues in this story. Katharine comments in her book, *Charles Stewart Parnell*, that some Irish people incorrectly called him Par*nell*, with the accent on the second syllable instead of the first.

# Family Tree of Charles Stewart Parnell (limited to those mentioned in book)

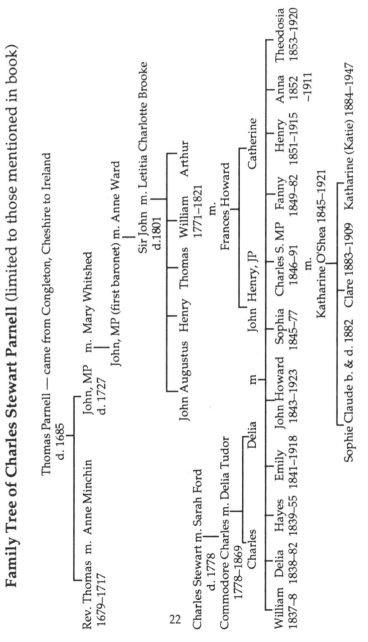

Thomas Parnell — came from Congleton, Cheshire to Ireland
d. 1685

Rev. Thomas  m.  Anne Minchin
1679–1717

John, MP  m.  Mary Whitshed
d. 1727

John, MP (first baronet) m. Anne Ward

Sir John  m.  Letitia Charlotte Brooke
d.1801

John Augustus  Henry  Thomas  William  Arthur
1771–1821

m.

Frances Howard

John Henry, JP  Catherine

m

Sophia  Charles S. MP  Fanny  Henry  Anna  Theodosia
1845–77  1846–91  1849–82  1851–1915  1852  1853–1920
                                              –1911

m.

Katharine O'Shea 1845–1921

Sophie  Claude b. & d. 1882  Clare 1883–1909  Katharine (Katie) 1884–1947

Charles Stewart m. Sarah Ford
d. 1778

Commodore Charles m. Delia Tudor
1778–1869

Charles    Delia

William  Delia  Hayes  Emily  John Howard  
1837–8  1838–82  1839–55  1841–1918  1843–1923

22

# Family Tree of Katharine Wood-O'Shea-Parnell (limited to those mentioned in book)

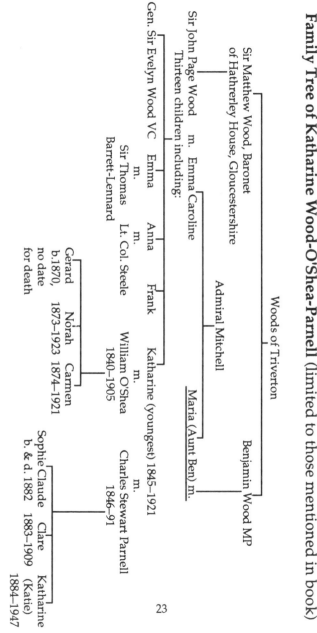

Sir Matthew Wood, Baronet
of Hathrerley House, Gloucestershire

Woods of Triverton

Sir John Page Wood    m.    Emma Caroline
Thirteen children including:

Admiral Mitchell

Benjamin Wood MP

Maria (Aunt Ben). m.

Gen. Sir Evelyn Wood VC    Emma    Anna    Frank    Katharine (youngest) 1845–1921

m.                          m.
Sir Thomas    Lt. Col. Steele
Barrett-Lennard

m.
William O'Shea
1840–1905

m.
Charles Stewart Parnell
1846–91

Gerard    Norah    Carmen
b.1870,    1873–1923    1874–1921
no date
for death

Sophie Claude    Clare    Katharine
b. & d. 1882    1883–1909    (Katie)
                               1884–1947

23

# 3

Katharine O'Shea was descended from the Wood family of Tiverton and her father, Sir John Page Wood, was the eldest son of Sir Matthew Wood. He studied at Winchester and at Trinity College, Cambridge, was appointed chaplain to Queen Caroline and attended her at her death in 1820. It was in this year also that he married eighteen-year-old Emma Caroline Mitchell, while he was still at Cambridge. Her sister, Maria, married Sir John's uncle, Benjamin Wood, MP for Southwark. Maria was Katharine's very wealthy Aunt Ben who was to play a pivotal role in the love affair of Katharine and Parnell.

Katharine was the youngest of thirteen children and was not born until the family moved from St. Peter's, Cornhill to Cressing in Essex. Shortly after her birth, they finally settled in a charming house in Riverhall Place, Glazenwood. The parents had a very small income which the mother augmented with her paintings — both miniatures and larger works — and she also had some stories published by Chapman and Hall.

While Katharine was still very young, her brother, Frank, who was in the army, invited herself and her sister, Anna, to visit him in Aldershot to see a review, and it was here that she first met Willie O'Shea who was in the 18th Hussars.

In time, Anna married Lieutenant Colonel Steele of the Lancers but the two soon parted, while another sister, Emma, married Sir Thomas Barrett-Lennard who had a country seat at Belhus. Willie O'Shea was a first class steeplechase rider and was invited to Belhus to ride a horse for Sir Thomas in the Brentwood Steeplechase. Too young to be launched into society, Katharine was escorted in to dinner by Willie. She said that she:

> ... was pleased with his youthful looks and vivacity. His dress pleased me also ... a brown velvet coat, cut rather fully, seal-

skin waistcoat, black-and-white check trousers, and an enormous carbuncle and diamond pin in his curiously folded scarf.

He was condescending at first, but the pair soon became friends, and saw much of each other over the following summer.

Willie's family were the O'Sheas of Limerick. His father, Henry, the eldest of three sons, inherited the heavily mortgaged family estate of Rich Hill. He qualified as a solicitor, made a fortune through property deals and cleared the family debt. He was married to Catherine Quinlan from Tipperary, and the couple had two children who were educated in England, France and Spain — Willie for whom the father purchased a commission in the 18th Hussars, and Mary who later became a Lady of the Royal Order of Theresa of Bavaria. Henry O'Shea had worked hard to make his money and indulged his son by saying that he should be a smart officer and 'do what other men do and send me the bill'.

After the meeting at Belhus, Willie and Katharine were constantly together over the next few years — indeed he seems to have been the only beau of any consequence that she had. In nature, all creatures guard their territory — including the human species — and when, on one occasion, Willie and Katharine were delivering a message to the officers at Purfleet and she received admiring glances, Willie kissed her full on the lips in public view, as he wanted 'to show those fellows that they must not make asses of themselves'.

In her book, Katharine describes some tender moments — when Willie was leaving to join his regiment, he gave her a rose and kissed her on the face and hair. Later, he had a riding accident and was unconscious for six weeks and, when he was being taken to Belhus to convalesce, being too weak to speak, he slipped a ring from his finger on to Katharine's. Shortly after this, he gave her a locket, which made her 'very happy to know how much Willie cared for me'. The courtship took over four years in all.

Katharine's father died in February 1866, leaving the family in bad financial straits. Her mother's sister, Maria, Mrs Benjamin Wood, whom Katharine called Aunt Ben, came to the rescue and settled a yearly income on Katharine's mother.

Meanwhile, Willie had taken his father's words at face value, and quickly ran up debts of £15,000 (£945,000). The indulgent father was not quite prepared for this recklessness and Willie was compelled to sell his army commission for £4,000 (£252,000), which he took over to Spain to invest in his uncle's bank. On his return to England, he told Katharine that he had waited for her for long enough, and so the pair were married in Brighton on 25 January 1867, nearly a year after her father's death. He was then twenty-seven years old and his young bride was just a week short of her twenty-second birthday.

It was a mixed marriage, Willie being a Roman Catholic and she Church of England. His mother and sister did not quite approve of the match but kindly gave Katharine 'beautiful Irish poplins to be made into gowns to impress the Spanish cousins, and a magnificent emerald bracelet, besides £200 (£12,600) worth of lovely Irish house linen'. After a honeymoon in England, the two set off for Madrid.

In the ideal marriage, the couple love and live happily ever after. Undoubtedly, Willie and Katharine shared this dream, but alas, due to unforeseen circumstances or human frailty, not all dreams survive. Less than a year after the marriage, Willie and his uncle fell out and the bank partnership was terminated. This was the first intimation to Katharine of money troubles which would haunt their marriage.

Returning to England, the O'Sheas started a stud farm at Bennington, Hertfordshire. Willie was no businessman and was slow to collect debts due. He started to gamble to relieve the financial position, but the debts mounted and he was declared a bankrupt just before the birth of their first child, Gerard, in 1870.

Over the following few years, the couple had two daughters, Norah and Carmen. The three children were baptised into the Catholic Church at Brompton Oratory. It is interesting to note Katharine's reaction to this in the light of later events.

After the birth of Norah, she took an interest in the Catholic religion and was instructed in it by a priest from the Oratory. She then considered the three members of her husband's family and their approach to their faith — Willie was a careless Catholic while the other two, she wrote, had such:

> ... fierce bigotry and deadly dullness of outlook, such an immense piety and so small charity, that my whole being revolted against such a belittling of God-given life ... and my excursion into the Catholic religion ended in abrupt revolt against all forms and creeds. This feeling was intensified when my second little girl Carmen, was born and christened at the Oratory. I would not go in, but stood waiting in the porch ... and I felt that my children were taken from me and that I was very lonely.

Aunt Ben helped with money as Willie's luck continued to fluctuate. He spent long periods away from the family, and Katharine and he began to drift apart. They lived in a series of houses, and eventually Aunt Ben gave Katharine a house in Eltham called Wonersh Lodge, whose ground backed on to her own fine residence — Eltham Lodge — while Willie went off to Spain for eighteen months to try his hand at the mining business.

Eltham itself was a very historic area, containing the remains of King John's palace which was lived in by the Plantagenet monarchs. The Tudors favoured the nearby Greenwich but Henry VIII spent long enough there to have drawn up the Eltham Statutes with Cardinal Wolsey in 1529. Included in these was the wise rule that 'Master cooks shall employ such scullions as shall not go about naked nor lie about all night before the kitchen fire'.

In 1648, Nathaniel Rich, on behalf of Cromwell, vandalised the palace. A wealthy vintner, Sir John Shaw, loaned some money to Charles II, was knighted for his services and given a pension of £500 a year. He settled in Eltham and built Eltham Lodge in 1665 in the English Renaissance style. Hugh May, a colleague of Christopher Wren, was the architect. The Shaw name can still be seen today, together with carved oak leaves (symbol of Charles II), in the mouldings above the fireplace in the dining room on the first floor. This room overlooked the old deer park. The main feature of the house is the decorated stairway. While the house was in the ownership of Aunt Ben, a tapestry (probably a gift from the king) in the billiard room was covered over. This was rediscovered at a much later date.

Aunt Ben's agreement with the O'Sheas was that Katharine would become her daily companion. The latter at all times did the bidding of this aunt who, from what we know of her, seems to have been a difficult old lady. Over the years, one of the few visitors to Eltham Lodge was the author, George Meredith, who was paid £300 (£18,900) a year (some books quote a smaller figure) to read to Aunt Ben — never his own works as she found them dull. Katharine tells us of a typical conversation:

'Now my dear lady, I will read you something of my own.'
'Indeed, Mr. Meredith, I cannot comprehend your works.'
'I will explain my meaning, dear Mrs. Wood.'
'You are prodigiously kind, dear Mr. Meredith, but I should prefer Molière to-day.'

When Aunt Ben aged even more and had no further interest in his readings, she gave Katharine the task of telling Meredith that his services were no longer required, without a thought as to whether the loss of the £300 would be a hardship to him.

Katharine's home, Wonersh Lodge, had three sitting rooms, a dining room and conservatory, a small garden at the front and a larger one at the back. Katharine was a good mother but, as Gerard was sent off to school at the age of eight, and the two girls had a nurse, she had much free time to socialise, which she did particularly in her aunt's house where she had a bedroom on the first floor.

Willie returned to England in 1880 and his old friend, The O'Gorman Mahon, suggested that he should enter political life. Aunt Ben, fearful that her idyllic life with Katharine would change, offered to pay the election expenses of both men and to set Willie up in an apartment in London. Willie could return at the weekends to see the family and take the children to Mass. Katharine would go to London to help Willie entertain for his political life if he was elected. The couple, though not very close, and having quarrelled on many occasions, were, nonetheless, on reasonable terms. Katharine had no great desire to have her husband at home constantly, and the arrangement seemed ideal.

So it was that, once more with Aunt Ben's financial help, Willie became part of the political scene. So it was that, when he was elected, he asked Katharine to help promote his position within the party by giving dinner parties. So it was that she and Parnell met.

# 4

After the success of the dinner/theatre party Katharine took to dropping in to the Ladies' Gallery in the House of Commons, to hear Parnell speak. Noticing her there, he would join her and, if the parliamentary discussion were not of great importance, the two would take a hansom cab and drive out into the country or to the river at Mortlake, which was almost in the opposite direction from Eltham. She said that these trips were because Willie wanted to secure Parnell's backing in case of another election, an unlikely eventuality as there had been an election just months before.

> While he sat by my side in the meadows by the river he promised he would do his best to keep Willie in Parliament ... Thus we would sit there through the summer afternoon, watching the gay traffic on the river, in talk, or in silence of tried friendship till the growing shadows warned us that it was time to drive back to London.

Her sister, Anna, gave a dinner party for four: Katharine and herself, Parnell and Justin McCarthy. Parnell escorted Katharine to the train afterwards and, when they discovered that it had left, hired a cab to drive her home.

The following Wednesday she went to Cannon Street Hotel to meet him. As there were some members of parliament around, he suggested they would be more 'comfortable' in his private sitting room. Here they enjoyed tea, political talk and long silences that she knew were 'dangerous in the complete sympathy they evoked between us'. Later that day, they had dinner at Thomas's Hotel before he left for Ireland.

No sooner had he arrived in Dublin than he wrote to her saying:

> I may tell you also something in confidence that I don't feel quite so content at the prospect of ten days' absence from

> London ... The cause is mysterious, but perhaps you will help
> me to find it, or her, on my return.

Meanwhile, the Government was still grappling with the Irish land problem — the solution of which was for many years a dream of Prime Minister Gladstone. When first asked to form a government in 1868, he had been at his home at Hawarden, where his favourite activity was tree felling, and it is reputed that his first statement was 'My mission is to pacify Ireland'. Notwithstanding these noble sentiments, peace had not been established between England and Ireland.

By 1880, evictions had increased in number and these provoked retaliation — in many cases violent retaliation. Parnell was opposed to any form of violence and on 19 September made a famous speech in Ennis, Co. Clare. He asked what should be done when someone bids for a farm after an eviction. The reply was that the bidder should be shot. Parnell suggested a different response:

> When a man takes a farm from which another has been unjustly evicted, you must shun him on the roadside when you meet him; you must shun him in the shop; you must shun him on the fair-green and in the market-place, and even in the place of worship, by leaving him alone; by putting him in a sort of moral Coventry; by isolating him from the rest of the country, as if he were a leper of old — you must show him your detestation of the crime he has committed.

The first person to be affected by this stratagem was a Captain Boycott in Co. Mayo. He could get no help locally and the cost of bringing in Orange labourers from the north to harvest his crops far outweighed the value of the work done. Eventually he had to leave. Thus the word 'boycotting' was added to the English language. The anti-violence system was to prove effective.

His work for the evicted people exhausted Parnell. He became quite ill and Willie invited him to stay with them at

Wonersh Lodge. Parnell had a morbid suspicion about the colour green and was convinced that Katharine's green carpet did not help his illness. A piece was analysed, but of course, was found to be harmless. Letters and parcels arrived for him, and once a week a box of eggs. He would not allow Katharine to use the eggs in case they had been poisoned.

The couple became even closer while she nursed him back to health. A change in the tone of his notes is noticeable by 17 October 1880 when he wrote:

> My own Love,
>
> You cannot imagine how much you have occupied my thoughts all day and how very greatly the prospect of seeing you again very soon comforts me....

And on 22 October:

> ... I send you the enclosed one or two poor sprigs of heather, which I plucked for you three weeks ago, also my best love, and hope you will believe that I always think of you as the one dear object whose presence has ever been a great happiness to me.

Around this time, he was visited by his friend, T.P. O'Connor, who said that Parnell was sensitive about going bald, then added, not without significance, 'perhaps it was the sensitiveness of a lover'. Parnell shaved his head and wore a skull cap in an attempt to have his hair grow thicker. It altered his appearance so completely that he was not recognised when he went to political meetings. If he noticed the stir he caused, he gave no sign.

Parnell toured Ireland speaking about the Land League at all sorts of venues, and tried to unite all sections of the Irish Party. Although he was a landowner himself, he spoke against payment of rent, and because his own tenants took his advice, he was left with little income. Willie O'Shea, also a landowner, did not appreciate his tactics.

Threats of prosecution, because of his utterances against government policy, reached Parnell and he was advised to go abroad for a while. One night he arrived at Wonersh Lodge and signalled his presence to Katharine at the sitting room window. He asked her if she could hide him for a fortnight, and that even the servants must not know his whereabouts. She had a little dressing-room with a sofa off her own room which she usually kept locked and she decided that it would be the ideal place. She cooked for him at night time and ordered a little extra on her own tray when her meals were served during the day. He had a complete fortnight's rest, which he spent writing speeches and reading *Alice in Wonderland!* When the fortnight had passed, Katharine got him out of the house unnoticed.

In no time, Parnell was back in the fray. Despite his plea for non-violent means, outrages continued and the Land League was blamed for these. Prosecutions began early in November 1880. Parnell wrote to Katharine on the fourth of that month: 'The thunderbolt, as you will have seen, has at last fallen, and we are in the midst of loyal preparations of a most appalling character'. The trials did not take place until after Christmas.

When Parnell thought that Willie was around, he always addressed the letters, 'My dear Mrs. O'Shea', and had them posted from other areas so that Willie would not know that he was in London. By 11 November, he had started to use another method — the official letter to her ran:

My dear Mrs. O'Shea,

I enclose keys, which I took away by mistake. Will you kindly hand enclosed letter to the proper person and oblige,

Yours very truly,

Chas. S. Parnell

The enclosed letter was also meant for her:

> My dearest Love,
>
> I have made all arrangements to be in London on Saturday morning, and shall call at Keppel Street for a letter from you. It is quite impossible for me to tell you just how very much you have changed my life, what a small interest I take in what is going on about me, and how I detest everything which has happened during the last few days to keep me away from you — I think of you always, and you must never believe there is any 'fading'. By the way, you must not send me any more artificial letters. I want as much of your own self as you can transfer into written words, or else none at all
>
> Yours always,
>
> C.S.P.
>
> P. S. A telegram goes to you, and one to W. [Willie] tomorrow, which are by no means strictly accurate.

Arguments have been put forward, in particular by Henry Harrison in his book, *Parnell Vindicated*, to show that Willie O'Shea knew of and encouraged the affair between his wife and Parnell. Harrison argues that Katharine's book was written in her old age, and that her son, Gerard (by Willie O'Shea), had an influence on her:

> ... as presented to the world it is a clumsy and self-revealing piece of partisanship in favour of the ousted husband whose supposed interests are fostered ruthlessly at the expense, not merely of the subject of the biography, but even of the unhappy authoress.

In the preface to her own book, Katharine comments on an article that gave a wrong impression of Parnell:

> Not a man who gave his country his whole life, and found the peace and courage of that life in the heart of the woman he loved. No, that is how a man lives and loves, whether in secret

or before the whole world. That is how Parnell lived and loved, and now after these long years I break my silence....

The letters she published were not the romancing of an old woman, but were Parnell's own, and it is clear from them that he did not want Willie to see their content. Why else would he put a letter within a covering letter when Willie was at home, and write freely when Willie was in Madrid? Why, if he was not covering his tracks when he visited Eltham, did he take a cab to the Old Kent Road, walk a little way and then take another cab for the last part of his journey?

Katharine writes that Willie was 'blind to the existence of the fierce, bewildering force that was rising within me in answer to the call of those passion-haunted eyes, that waking or sleeping never left me.' She continues:

HIS wife could not love anyone but himself; perhaps unfortunately she did not even do that, but after all 'love' was only a relative term — a little vulgar even, after girlhood had passed, and the mild affection of his own feelings towards her were no doubt reciprocated, in spite of the unfortunate temperamental differences that made constant companionship impossible.

Katharine and Willie had quarrelled and lived apart for long and short periods of time but the relationship was not broken off. The fact that their first ardent passion had faded after so many years of marriage was in no doubt, but he still thought of her as his property.

Most of the male biographers say that Katharine loved Parnell with passion and that, under those circumstances, it would be physically impossible for her to have anything more to do with Willie. Yet they would agree that many a man has an affair, passionate or otherwise, and, for many reasons, does not break completely with his wife. Similarly, when Katharine first met Parnell, she and Willie were not having an ardent sex life — they were rarely together — but, however distasteful she found it, she would have to continue with their arrangement in order to conceal the affair.

Parnell and Katharine were both very much in love; from very early in their relationship to the day of his death, he thought of her as his wife and would have married her immediately if she had divorced Willie. She says that at first she fought against Parnell's love: 'I urged my children and his work'. She was a devoted mother and would not agree to leave her children. Parnell's political life might suffer. Without doubt, however, one of the overriding objections to divorce was money. Katharine, Willie and Parnell had little or no money between them, yet all three liked to live well. Aunt Ben had a considerable fortune and provided Katharine and Willie with separate housing and incomes, as well as paying for the children's nurses and education. A letter from Willie to Chamberlain in 1892 says that the aunt:

> ... allowed my former wife about £4,000 [£252,000] a year but often, and especially in 1882, I was in want of money... and I certainly pressed my former wife to keep her aunt up to her promises.

In time, Aunt Ben promised her 'Swan', as she called Katharine, that she would be her heir. Willie hoped for his share of the inheritance. As long as Katharine stayed at Wonersh Lodge and visited daily, all was well. Aunt Ben would not take kindly to the scandal of a divorce, but she *was* very old and not expected to last long.

Katharine's lifestyle gave her ample time to be with Parnell, under the cover of politics, while Willie troubled her very little. None of the parties involved was particularly religious, and repeatedly in her book Katharine says that there was quite a degree of infidelity in society: the rule was not to be found out. In the preface to her book, she writes:

> And because Parnell contravened certain social laws, not regarding them as binding him in any way, and because I joined him in this contravention since his love made all else of no

account to me, we did not shrink at the clamour of the up-
holders of those outraged laws, nor resent the pressing of the
consequences that were inevitable and always foreseen. The
freedom of choice we had ourselves claimed we acknowledged
for others, and were wise enough to smile if, in some instances,
the greatness of our offence was loudly proclaimed by those
who he knew lived a freedom of love more varied than our
own.

# 5

Parnell spent Christmas 1880 — this time officially — at Eltham, and returned to Ireland immediately afterwards. Having checked that Willie had gone to Madrid, he wrote on 28 December:

> My dearest Wife,
>
> You will be delighted to learn that everything is proceeding first rate so far.
> The jury sworn to-day cannot possibly convict us, and there is a very fair chance of an acquittal. I do not think the Government will attempt to prevent me from being present at the opening of Parliament....

In his letters, he was by now claiming Katharine as his wife:

> For good or ill, I am your husband, your lover, your children, your all. And I will give my life to Ireland, but to you I give my love, whether it be in your heaven or your hell. It is destiny. When I first looked into your eyes I knew.

While there is no letter to prove this last avowal, and it is Katharine's own account, words along this line must, indeed, have been said.

In January, Willie formed the totally groundless suspicion that Katharine was having him followed by a detective. He arrived at Eltham unexpectedly and had words with his wife. Naturally, she denied any misdemeanour, but when Willie went upstairs he found Parnell's portmanteau in the room next to Katharine's. Enraged, he left the house, taking the portmanteau which he threw out at Charing Cross Station, vowing he would shoot Parnell in a duel. If he had condoned the affair, would he have issued such a challenge?

On 7 January 1881, Parnell innocently wrote asking where he could find his luggage. Willie proposed they fight the duel:

> Will you be kind enough to be in Lille or any other town in
> the north of France which may suit your convenience on
> Saturday next 16th inst. Please let me know by one o'clock
> p.m. where to expect you. I await your answer and am
> arranging with a friend to accompany me.

Parnell accepted but calmly added that, after the duel, he
would be obliged if he could still see Mrs O'Shea as he was
using her as a means of communication between himself and
Gladstone.

At Westminster Hotel, Anna Steele confronted Parnell
about the affair. He assured her there were no grounds for
the suspicions. She persuaded Willie to go back to Eltham
with her, where, according to the subsequent divorce report:
'... there was a stormy and terrible scene — The result however was that there was a reconciliation and they resumed
their former relations'. Willie withdrew his challenge but
made it a condition that Parnell would visit Eltham only
when 'the exigencies of the political situation' required it.

Katharine writes that, 'From the date of this bitter quarrel
Parnell and I were one, without further scruple, without
fear, and without remorse'. Again Harrison uses this to sus-
tain his argument that she was on bad terms with Willie
from then on. Willie had, however, withdrawn the challenge.

The proceedings of the long awaited conspiracy trial of
the Land League leaders had started on 28 December 1880,
and large demonstrations were held in favour of the
accused. On 23 January, the case, predictably, collapsed as
the jury could not agree. To help with expenses, a Parnell
Defence Fund was opened and many Catholic clergy
contributed. £21,000 (£1,323,000) was collected. The Irish
parties seemed more united than ever.

On 31 January 1881, a debate began on the proposed
Protection of Person and Property Bill which gave powers to
imprison without trial anyone suspected of engaging in un-
lawful activities. On 7 April, Gladstone introduced his
second Land Bill which, although it was not perfect, gave

tenants joint ownership with the landlords, of their holdings. This pleased the more moderate Irish sections including the clergy, while the small farmers and the Fenians rejected it. Parnell could not afford to alienate either side and advised his followers to abstain. He decided to bring test cases to court to see if the rents were fair, to please the moderates, and made a series of provocative speeches to please the extremists.

Throughout that year, Parnell and Katharine kept in touch through coded letters. He addressed her as 'My own Wifie', 'My own Loveliest', 'My dearest Katie', and wrote, 'Your King thinks very often of his dearest Queen', signing himself 'Your own loving King' or 'Your loving Husband'.

Despite Willie's curtailments on visits to Eltham, they met constantly. In May 1881, Aunt Ben had a visit from a friend, and Katharine and the children were able to get away for a while to Brighton. Parnell joined them there unexpectedly and was unrecognisable when he arrived as he had himself cut off his beard, and wore a white muffler. He booked into an hotel under the name of 'Stewart'. It was a very happy time for them and it was then that she conceived his first child. (In a letter from Kilmainham Gaol, dated 14 February 1882, he finishes: 'When I get out I hope to have a good long rest with my own little Wifie somewhere, and to listen to the waves breaking as we used those mornings of spring last May'.)

Throughout that summer, they were together as much as possible. The threat of his imprisonment was a constant worry. Katharine writes:

> ... I felt an unreasonable fear and loneliness when he was away from me. He was very tender and considerate to me, but pointed out that the turmoil and rebellion he had brought to a head in Ireland must be very carefully handled to be product-ive of ultimate good, and that he could 'mark time' with the Land Leaguers better in Kilmainham than out.

And elsewhere:

> I was not strong and I was full of anxiety as to the probable effects upon Parnell's health of life in Kilmainham Gaol. In addition to my anxiety, the deception I had to practise towards Captain O'Shea, seldom as I saw him, told upon my nerves just now.

Although the *Nation* and the *Freeman's Journal* gave him sympathetic coverage, Parnell felt that he needed to have complete control of a newspaper. With £3,000 (£189,000), for the most part subscribed in America, he bought three run down papers — the *Shamrock*, *Flag of Ireland* and the *Irishman* — from Richard Pigott, a journalist with a dubious reputation. Parnell casually signed the usual letters of purchase which would be used at a later date for a completely unforeseen purpose. The new newspaper was called *United Ireland* and a twenty-eight-year-old man, William O'Brien, was engaged as editor. The first edition was published on 13 August 1881.

William O'Brien had first met Parnell on a train in November 1878, and wrote of him:

> He has captured me, heart and soul, and is bound to go on capturing ... a delicate reserve, without the smallest suspicion of hauteur; strangest of all, humour; above all else simplicity... a man one could suffer with proudly.

On 25 September 1881, Parnell made a speech in Dublin which was welcomed with a torch-light procession and was the greatest demonstration since Daniel O'Connell's time. Foster, the Chief Secretary, urged Gladstone to arrest the leaders of the Land League. On 7 October, Gladstone answered with a speech in Leeds:

> He says that until he has submitted his test cases any farmer who pays his rent is a fool. It is a dangerous thing for a man to be denounced as a fool by the head of the most violent party in the country....

To this Parnell replied at Wexford on 9 October:

It is a good sign that this masquerading knight-errant ... should be obliged to throw off the mask today, and stand revealed as the man who, by his own utterances, is prepared to carry fire and sword into your homesteads, unless you humbly abase yourselves before him and before the landlords of the country.

This could not continue. Time was running out for Parnell and he said that, if he were arrested, 'Captain Moonlight' would take over.

A terrible gale and storm raged around Eltham on 13 October, when Willie arrived from London with the news of Parnell's arrest. Katharine received a letter from Morrison's Hotel in Dublin:

My own Queenie,

I have just been arrested by two fine looking detectives, and write these words to wifie to tell her that she must be a brave little woman and not fret after her husband.

The only thing that makes me worried and unhappy is that it may hurt you and our child.

You know, darling, that on this account it will be wicked of you to grieve, as I can never have any other wife but you, and if anything happens to you I must die childless. Be good and brave, dear little wifie, then.

Your Own Husband.

Politically it is a fortunate thing for me that I have been arrested, as the movement is breaking fast, and all will be quiet in a few months, when I shall be released.

# 6

On 13 October 1881, Gladstone, while speaking at the Guild-hall, was handed a telegram. He announced:

> I have been informed that ... the first step has been taken in the arrest of the man who has made himself pre-eminent in the attempt to destroy that authority of the law, and substitute what would end in nothing more nor less than anarchical oppression exercised upon the people of Ireland....

Riots took place in Dublin while most of the British Government rejoiced.

Arrested soon after Parnell were Thomas Sexton and the acting secretary of the League, P.J. Quinn. John Dillon, recently released, took over briefly as head of the League, but was re-arrested. J.J. O'Kelly and O'Brien joined them, and Parnell greeted the latter: 'O'Brien, of all men in the world, you are the man we wanted'.

He was invited to draw up a manifesto asking tenants 'to pay no rents under any circumstances to their landlords until the government relinquishes the existing system of terrorism and restores the constitutional rights of the people'. This was signed by Parnell, Brennan, Kettle, Geston, Dillon — all in Kilmainham Gaol — and the names of Michael Davitt, then in Portland Prison, and Patrick Egan, in Paris at the time, were added.

On 18 October, the manifesto was made public but was condemned by the Catholic Church, even by Archbishop Croke of Cashel, the most sympathetic towards the agitation. Two days later, the government suppressed the League. Chaos resulted: some tenants paid their rent or tested it in the courts; others reacted violently.

Meanwhile, those arrested settled into life in the prison. As described by William O'Brien in *The Parnell of Real Life*, the inmates were allowed to gather together for long periods to play chess, dominoes and handball, read newspapers or smoke. Meals were supplied by a local restaurateur. In a letter of 7 January 1882, Parnell writes:

> I am being fed very well. Chops or grilled turkey or eggs and bacon for breakfast, soup and chops for luncheon, and joint and vegetables, etc. for dinner, and sometimes oysters. The 'one meal a day' is only a pretence.

Each brought his own particular talents to the company and Parnell delighted in talking about America.

As green was the colour associated with Ireland many gifts of that colour were sent to Parnell, including a beautiful quilt. He had a horror of the colour and disposed of each and every one of them. His superstitions also ran to a hatred of the number 13 and its multiples.

It did not take long to find a way of getting letters to and from Katharine. A day after his arrest, he wrote:

> I am very comfortable here, and have a beautiful room facing the sun — the best in the prison. There are three or four of the best of the men in adjoining rooms with whom I can associate all day long, so that time does not hang heavy nor do I feel lonely. My only fear is about my darling Queenie. I have been racked with torture all to-day, last night, and yesterday, lest the shock may have hurt you or our child. Oh darling, write or wire me as soon as you get this that you are well and will try not to be unhappy until you see your husband again. You may wire me here. I have your beautiful face with me here [He had a locket with her photograph with him]; it is such a comfort. I kiss it every morning.
>
> Your King.

Meanwhile, Katharine was successfully playing a double role. Willie, thinking the expected child was his, called often to Eltham to enquire after his wife's health, and looked forward to the birth in February 1882 as he felt it would bring them together again —this was the last thing she desired.

On 16 February, Katharine gave birth to a brown-eyed

baby girl. The infant seemed healthy at first and Parnell wrote: 'I shall love her very much better than if it had been a son'. Within two months the little girl's health deteriorated rapidly and Katharine was heartbroken. Surprisingly, she speaks kindly of Willie: 'Willie was very good; I told him my baby was dying and I must be left alone. He had no suspicion of the truth, and only stipulated that the child should be baptised at once'. The child's birth being registered as O'Shea, there was little choice but to baptise her into the Catholic religion. Parnell had no objection although he was Church of Ireland, but it must have been a greater problem for Katharine with her avowed dislike of any creed, particularly Catholicism. At a ceremony in the house at Eltham, the infant was given the name Sophie Claude. Maybe Willie did not know that Parnell's sister was also called Sophie.

Shortly before the child died, Parnell was given parole for the funeral in Paris of his twenty-year-old nephew, Henry, only son of his sister, Delia. On his way, he called to Eltham and Katharine was greatly consoled when she could put the baby in his arms. As a conciliatory gesture, he wired Willie to expect him at Eltham on the way back, and they talked politics long into the night. Katharine says that, early on 22 April, '... my little one died as my lover stole in to kiss us both and say good-bye'.

A letter from the O'Shea in-laws to Katharine seems to prove that they never suspected the child was not Willie's. According to F.S.L. Lyons, another letter, of 25 April, from Willie to Joseph Chamberlain, included the line: 'My child is to be buried at Chislehurst this afternoon'.

Soon after Parnell returned to prison, an agreement, known as the Kilmainham Treaty, was reached with the British Government, and Willie was instrumental in this. In it Parnell promised to pacify the country and to co-operate with the Liberals, they promised to drop coercion, release the prisoners, amend the Land Act, and to help tenants to pay arrears. Parnell and his followers were released on 2 May 1882.

# 7

Chief Secretary W.E. Foster did not agree with the Kilmainham Treaty and resigned in protest. His successor, Lord Frederick Cavendish, arrived in Dublin on 6 May 1882. That very evening, he and the Under Secretary, Mr Thomas Henry Burke, were murdered by an extremist group called the Invincibles. Around six o'clock, Lord Cavendish left Dublin Castle to walk to the Phoenix Park. Burke, travelling by cab, caught up on him and dismissed the cab to join him. James Carey, who was to identify the victims, saw the two men and signalled to a group of men waiting opposite the Viceregal Lodge. The assassins approached — three, followed by two and a further two. As the first three passed by, a man called Brady quickly stabbed Burke. Lord Cavendish tried to help Burke, but he too was stabbed. Finally, the throats of the two men were cut. The murder had taken just three minutes and many passers-by had no idea of what had happened. Carey later turned informer but was himself assassinated in his turn as he left Ireland by boat.

Parnell, who had travelled to see Katharine after his release from prison, was deeply shocked at the outrage and considered resigning. He was on his way to meet Davitt and others when he saw the news in the *Sunday Observer*. Katharine wired Willie to bring Parnell home to Eltham for dinner, and both pleaded with him not to resign, a plea later echoed by Gladstone. Parnell made a speech in the House of Commons, denouncing the crime.

Michael Davitt and John Dillon joined him in signing a manifesto a day later:

To the People of Ireland

— On the eve of what seemed a bright future for our country, that evil destiny which has apparently pursued us for centuries has struck another blow at our hopes, which cannot be exaggerated in its disastrous consequence....

Surprisingly, the situation turned to Parnell's advantage: the extremists, who would have condemned the Kilmainham Treaty, were discredited because they were associated with the Invincibles; and a harsher Coercion Bill united the Irish. Parnell, instead of reviving the Land League, in October 1882, founded the National League which was under his control, marking a phase in which he was the undisputed leader of nationalism in Ireland.

While Parnell had been in prison, Anna, his sister, had been very active in the Ladies' Land League, which had become very extremist in outlook. Her brother disapproved thoroughly and stopped all funds to this organisation, bringing about its closure. To his death, Anna would never forgive him for this action.

As he and Willie were politically interdependent, Parnell was again accepted as a house guest at Eltham. Shortly after the founding of the National League, Parnell fell ill with a cold following an attack of 'dysenteric diarrhoea'. Attacks of this kind were frequent and Katharine always nursed him back to health. She herself was taking things easy, having again become pregnant in June 1882, a month after his release from prison.

That year, the Arrears Act assisted 130,000 tenants to pay off their arrears with money from the Church Surplus Fund. Gladstone needed the support of the Irish vote and used Katharine as an intermediary between himself and Parnell. In her description of her meetings with Gladstone, she tells of how, when she came into his room, he insisted on closing all doors to prevent anybody from hearing their conversation. The two would pace up and down the room exchanging messages, and he always treated her with charm and made her feel she was playing an important political role. In the preface to her book she writes:

I did not once throughout those eleven years attempt to use

> my influence over him [Parnell] to 'bias' his public life or pol-
> itics ... In my many interviews with Mr. Gladstone I was
> Parnell's messenger, and in all other work ... it was under-
> stood on both sides that I worked for Parnell alone.

Parnell was acutely short of money in 1882 and when his
mother, on a trip to America, appealed for financial help, he
was unable to send her any. Avondale was mortgaged for
£13,000 (£819,000) and this had been foreclosed, so he filed
for a petition to sell it. He had a good friend in Archbishop
Croke of Cashel who, on reading this news in the newspapers, suggested that the Irish should start a fund to pay off
the mortgage. Nearly £8,000 (£504,000) was at first contributed, but the Vatican instructed the Irish hierarchy to put an
end to it. Although the bishops and priests had to obey, the
public within five weeks increased their contribution and, by
December, the fund amounted to £37,000 (£2,331,000). Gladstone noted that the Pope had little effect on Irish politics.

On 11 December, the Lord Mayor of Dublin presented
Parnell with a cheque for the amount collected. According to
R. Barry O'Brien, Parnell made a speech on the general situation, saying nothing about the cheque. Lord Spencer wrote:
'he made a long speech, but never said a word about the
cheque ... and he gives offence to nobody. That little incident always made an impression on me, because it showed
the immense power of the man'.

However, on the advice of his party, he later said a short
but pointed few words of gratitude:

> I don't know how adequately to express my feelings with
> regard not only to your lordship's address, not only to the
> address to the Parnell National Tribute, but also with regard to
> the magnificent demonstration. I prefer to leave to the historian
> the description of tonight and the expression of opinion as
> regards the result which tonight must produce.

F.S.L. Lyons suggests that:

> Reticent about his private affairs to an extreme degree, the

48

mere business of receiving a gift of money to set right his financial position can only have been deeply humiliating to him, and his clipped remarks to the Lord Mayor and to the Rotunda audience were almost certainly the reaction of a highly embarrassed man.

1883 saw the building of cottages for labourers under the Labourers' Act, and it was a time of great joy for Katharine and Parnell with the birth in March of their daughter, Clare. Surprisingly, Katharine does not mention this child in her biography, but Clare, like little Sophie Claude, was baptised a Catholic and bore the name of O'Shea. For most of 1884, Katharine was again pregnant.

The Reform Act of 1884 more than trebled the electorate as all householders acquired the right to vote, bringing the Irish system in line with its counterpart in England. From December 1884 to March 1885, Parnell toured Ireland, canvassing for the newly acquired votes, and gained an extra ten seats in the 1885 election.

In January 1885, he went to Cork to stay with his old friend, Michael J. Horgan. Crowds meeting him at the railway station, taking the horses from the carriage, drew it to the Horgan home. That night, on the eve of the election, he spoke in the Cork Opera House. His speech included the memorable lines which, in letters of bronze, now adorn his monument in O'Connell Street, Dublin:

No man has a right to fix the boundary to the march of a nation. No man has a right to say to his country: 'Thus far shalt thou go and no further'. We have never attempted to fix the *ne plus ultra* to the progress of Ireland's nationhood and we never shall.

That night he was invited to give a talk on Irish history to the Young Ireland Society. He admitted to Horgan that he knew little about the subject, and borrowed some books fifteen minutes before the lecture was to start.When he arrived at the venue an hour and a half late and was loudly cheered for his speech. Horgan was decidedly nervous and said:

> He did not seem to have the faintest notion that people looked
> up to him, not only as the greatest man in Ireland, but one of the
> most remarkable men in Europe. He spoke like a young man
> making his debut at a debating society ... Yet with all his self-
> deprecation, modesty and gentleness you always felt that you
> were in the presence of a master.

The election over, the Liberals were split on the question of
coercion. Willie O'Shea was used by Chamberlain to take to
Parnell his plan to let the Irish help run their own affairs.
This suggested that elected county councils could take over
some of the work of Dublin Castle. Parnell agreed but sent
the message back, again via Willie, that it should not replace
the campaign for Home Rule. Willie did not make this plain
to Chamberlain who thought that Parnell had accepted his
suggestion in full as a solution to the Irish demands. Parnell's position was publicised, Chamberlain felt betrayed
and bad feeling was aroused. The divisions between the two
brought about the defeat of Gladstone's Parliament on 8
June 1885.

Because the reorganisation of constituencies had not taken
place after the Reform Act, a caretaker government was
formed, with Lord Salisbury as Prime Minister, which needed the Irish votes to stay in power. This gave Parnell a very
strong hand. Coercion was dropped and the position of Lord
Lieutenant was given to a man who was sympathetic to
Home Rule — Lord Carnarvon.

Parnell started to play one party against the other, in an
attempt to get the best deal for Ireland. At first, Lord Carnarvon declared himself in favour of independence for Ireland but, unknown to Parnell, this was not the feeling of all
the Conservatives. With Gladstone afraid to split the Liberal
vote by showing himself to be in favour of Home Rule, Parnell decided to ask the Irish in England not to vote for
Gladstone's party in the election. However, the Liberals won
by 86 seats — just the number of the Irish party. He could
combine with the Conservatives, but he had lost the balance
of power.

# 8

Parnell's private life was well hidden from his followers. According to T.P. O'Connor, for nearly ten years not a single member of his party, with the possible exception of his secretary, knew his address.

A young woman named Jane Glenister went into service at Wonersh Lodge in October 1880 for two years and was subsequently to be a witness in the divorce proceedings. She said that at first Captain O'Shea was at the lodge 'most of the time' and Parnell was a visitor. She accompanied the family to Brighton in the spring of 1881 and said that, when they returned to Eltham, Parnell was there 'a great deal'. He occupied the bedroom separated from Mrs O'Shea's by a drawing room with inter-connecting doors. On one occasion, the doors were locked, but Mrs O'Shea told her that there was a 'secret society about and it was necessary for the doors to be locked'. She was told that if anyone asked if Parnell was in the house she was to say 'No'.

Around this time, Brighton Railway Station was being rebuilt. Parnell had a great interest in architectural design and spent hours observing the construction of the new roof to the station. He would estimate the measurements of the height and depth of the span by pacing them and, returning home, would draw what he had seen. He used these plans to have a cattle shed constructed at Avondale on similar lines.

At the end of 1883, Katharine thought about taking a house in Brighton or Hove. She had arranged to go to Second Avenue but Willie persuaded her that Medina Terrace, Hove, would be better as it was facing the sea. Parnell came to stay as he wanted to discuss the Local Government Bill with Willie and to find out Chamberlain's views. Katharine came and went, as she had to keep an eye on Aunt Ben. She was with her aunt on Christmas Eve, when Parnell came to join her. Aunt Ben, who never liked Christmas celebrations, was shut away in her warm house.

Parnell and Katharine walked together by moonlight up and down the snow-covered wide terrace, listening to the local band accompanying the carol singers. As they were near King John's palace, she told him that the shadows on the snow were the ghosts of King John's hunters, while he explained his belief in predestination, and that some souls, united in life, were parted in death 'by the second planet life', until 'sheer longing for one another brought them together again'. They stood together at midnight to listen to the ringing of bells in many surrounding villages.

These romantic encounters had, nevertheless, to be hidden away from the eyes of the public and also from Willie. Parnell visited Katharine at Medina Terrace in Hove (sometimes referred to as West Brighton), under the name of Charles Stewart and always arrived via the beach entrance with a cloth cap down over his eyes. They would drive out at night time — never by day — and spent most of their time locked in a room.

In March 1884, Willie went to Lisbon and Madrid and, on his return, apparently suspecting nothing, he went over to visit Avondale with Parnell. Katharine published a letter from Parnell in Avondale, dated 30 May 1884, in which he wrote: 'Captain and I arrived safely'.

Willie eventually heard rumours and, although Katharine was quite pregnant at the time, he wrote to Parnell on 4 August:

> You have behaved very badly to me. While I have often told you that you were welcome to stay at Eltham whenever I was there, I begged of you not to do so during my absence, since it would be sure at least, sooner or later, to cause a scandal. I am making arrangements with a view to taking my family abroad for a long time, and I hope that they will be sufficiently advanced to allow of my asking for the Chiltern Hundreds before the end of the session.

Willie seemed prepared to forego Aunt Ben's fortune and also to give up his own political career.

Parnell replied:

> I do not know of any scandal, or any ground for one, and can only suppose that you have misunderstood the drift of some statements that may have been made about me.

Katharine wrote to Willie:

> I am very sorry that you should have worries on my account but after our conversation on Tuesday I could not imagine you would expect me. In any case I was feeling scarcely strong enough to travel again in the heat and for the children's sake I should not like to die yet.

In November, Katharine (Katie), Parnell's third child, was born and was given the O'Shea name and religion.

Early the following year, a new room was added to the back of Wonersh Lodge. Parnell supervised the work and brought over sweet chestnut timber from Avondale for panelling and other woodwork as the room was to be used by him as a study. It was connected to Katharine's boudoir, and he had his own latch key made so that he could let himself in through this new entrance.

Katharine's eldest child, Gerard, was fifteen years of age by now and, for the first time, began to take note of Parnell's comings and goings.

In February 1885, Parnell's horses — Dictator, which Katharine used, and his own mount, President — were brought over to Eltham to be stabled. In time, a third horse, Home Rule, joined them, but he was not a very good animal. Parnell also brought over from Ireland an Irish setter called Grouse who was devoted to both of them and was happiest when they sat with clasped hands so that he could rest his head on both of his adored owners. Pincher, a half-starved mongrel terrier was the next to join the menagerie and was returned to full health with tender loving care. An old setter, Ranger, completed the trio of dogs.

In April 1885, the Prince of Wales was to visit Ireland, and

Katharine and Parnell jokingly wondered if he would be made welcome or otherwise — she threatening to hang Union Jacks from the windows in Avondale if he made things unpleasant for the Prince. Parnell advised the Irish public to treat the visitors with polite indifference. This advice was followed in Dublin but not in other places. In Cork, for example, black flags were hung out or waved by the public, while rotten eggs and cabbages were thrown at the Royal party.

Meanwhile, Willie O'Shea was deluding himself as to his own importance to the political life of the day. He wrote in May to Katharine:

> To-day C. [Chamberlain] promised me the Chief Secretaryship on the formation of the government after the election ... This is an enormous thing, giving you and the chicks a very great position....

While Willie was away, Katharine and Parnell continued to see each other. They would go out late at night, even as late as midnight or 1 o'clock. When the family moved to the seaside, they came back on their own to Wonersh Lodge.

# 9

At the end of 1885, as lawlessness in Ireland increased, the government moved towards dissolution. A rift was beginning to develop between Parnell and some of his followers, led by Healy, who felt that he was neglecting his work for Ireland. Word of this reached Chamberlain.

Elections were afoot in January 1886. Willie was put forward unsuccessfully for mid-Armagh. When T.P. O'Connor won two seats — one in the Scottish division and one in Galway — Willie, who had been useful in dealings with Chamberlain, felt that his work should be rewarded. Chamberlain wrote to Willie on 22 January:

> Surely it must be to the interest of the Irish party to keep open channels of communication with the Liberal leaders? Can you not get Mr. Parnell's exequatur for one of the vacant seats? It is really the least he can do for you, after all you have done for him....

Katharine, too, urged Parnell to help: 'I was very anxious that Willie should remain in parliament. Politics were a great interest to him and gave him little time to come down to Eltham'. Parnell decided to propose Willie for the Galway seat and, to strengthen his proposal, said he would resign himself if Willie were not accepted as the candidate — a threat he later withdrew.

The nationalists did not want Willie to represent them as he had never taken their pledge and always refused to sit with them in parliament. Healy and Biggar believed the stories that Parnell and Katharine were lovers, but neither said it to his face nor referred to it in public. Katharine writes that a member of the party opened a letter from her to Parnell but does not say who or when. Secretly, Healy and Biggar hinted that Willie knew of and encouraged his wife's liaison with the Chief, and that this was why Parnell supported him. Biggar intended to send Parnell a telegram saying 'Mrs. O'Shea will be your ruin', but Healy persuaded him to change this to 'The O'Sheas will be your ruin'.

Other party members did not believe the rumours. T.P. O'Connor wrote:

> To no human being did he [Parnell] ever breathe the remotest allusion to this dark reverse of his great and prosperous life. He made it an argument against his friends ... that they knew of the intrigue for years. The argument was both unjust and ungenerous. There, of course, was plenty of suspicion but there was no proof, and respect for his feelings, the awe in which everybody stood of him, the distance which he always placed between himself and even his closest friends — all this prevented anything like an allusion to the subject.

It was surely a combination of Katharine's urgings, and of wanting to keep open the lines of communication to Chamberlain, that prompted Parnell to insist on O'Shea, but the latter was, of course, the reason given to the party. His opponents favoured Michael Lynch and Healy made it quite clear that, if O'Shea were forced upon them, he would say that the Irish party had not been consulted. This was reported in the press on 8 February and was countered a day later in the *Freeman's Journal*:

> The issue is not between Captain O'Shea and Mr. Lynch but whether at the very moment of the crisis, when the question of Home Rule hangs in the balance, when Mr. Parnell almost holds it in the hollow of his hand, Galway will strike a blow at his prestige and his authority.

Party members were asked to declare support for the leader.

When Parnell arrived in Galway, he was accompanied by T.P. O'Connor, who had caused the vacancy in the first place and who had at first opposed O'Shea but had later rallied behind his chief. They were taken aback to be greeted at the station by cries from a hostile crowd of 'To hell with O'Shea' or 'To hell with Parnell'. The mob, afraid of their leader, focused their attention on O'Connor, but Parnell steered him towards the hotel. A private meeting was held and it became clear that Parnell had the support of the vast majority. He then addressed the public, who were soon on his side once again. Lynch was told that O'Shea was to be the candidate. The former could not, however, withdraw, so he decided not to canvass. Support for Parnell was shown by the electorate when O'Shea received 942 votes against Lynch's 54.

The Galway mutiny, as it was called, was put down — but at great cost. The split in the party would remain hidden as long as Parnell would deliver on Home Rule. Contact with Gladstone was made through John Morley in March 1886. In the words of Morley:

> Mr. Parnell showed himself acute, frank, patient, closely attentive, and possessed of striking though not rapid insight. He never slurred over difficulties, nor tried to pretend that rough was smooth ... He measured the ground with a slow and careful eye, and fixed tenaciously on the thing that was essential at the moment. Of constructive faculty he never showed a trace. He was a man of temperament of will, of authority, of power; not of ideas or ideals, or knowledge, or political maxims, or even of the practical reason in any of its higher senses ... But he knew what he wanted.

There was no doubt that what Parnell wanted was Home Rule. He made it clear that he would not mind if the Irish had to withdraw from Westminster as they 'would want all the brains they had for their own parliament', but he would like it accepted that a delegation might be sent if Irish questions arose. Right up to 5 April he pressed his points home. On this date, he spent two hours with Morley. They were joined at 10.30 p.m. by Gladstone, who greeted Parnell cordially and sat between him and Morley to continue the discussion. Parnell was, according to Morley, 'extraordinarily close, tenacious and sharp'. He continues:

> At midnight Mr. Gladstone rose in his chair and said 'I fear I must go; I cannot sit as late as I used to do' and 'Very clever,

> very clever' he muttered to me as I held open the door of his room for him. I returned to Parnell, who went on repeating his points in his impenetrable way, until the policeman mercifully came to say the House was up.

On 8 April 1886, Gladstone moved the first reading of the Home Rule Bill. It was followed eight days later by the Land Bill — which proposed to buy out the landlords, and was quickly opposed by the latter.

Taking a break, Katharine took the children to the Queen's Hotel in Eastbourne, where Parnell joined them. They decided to rent a house and contacted Samuel Drury, a property owner, who made out an agreement, signed by Katharine, to take a house on St. John's Road for two months. The agreement was extended to nineteen weeks, and Thomas Kennett was engaged as a page.

Parnell loved the sea, but Katharine was not strong enough to join in his swimming. One day he persuaded her to wade, fully clothed, into the waves with him:

> He held me tightly, laughing aloud as the ripple of waves and wind caught my hair and loosed it about my shoulders; and, as I grew cold and white, my wonderful lover carried me, with all my weight of soaked clothing, back to the shore, kissing the wet hair that the wind twisted about his face and whispering the love that almost frightened me in its strength.

With Parnell having to make trips to London and Ireland, and Katharine having to make flying visits to ensure that Aunt Ben was all right, they decided to bring down Parnell's horses under the charge of Thomas Partridge, the stable boy from Eltham. Parnell would go for a morning ride on his horse, President, and in the afternoon, Partridge would harness up the phaeton and Katharine would join Parnell for drives around Eastbourne.

The favourite trip was to Birling Gap, where the horse would be tied up and left for over an hour with a sulking Thomas, while the pair would visit their friend, the coastguard, to hear his sea stories, or would just stroll around listening to the sea and the birds. This became more exciting when a storm blew up, causing the sea to thunder and the gales to scream around them. As the sea raged, he would wrap her in his coat and exclaim, 'Isn't this glorious, My Queen? Isn't it alive?'

They planned to build a dream house there or to take over a partly-built one at Beachy Head. Buildings always excited him and he inspected every inch of the house. It was at Beachy Head that Parnell, while he rolled the lawns of the partly-built house, dictated to Katharine, who sat on the steps, his Constitution for the English and Irish Peoples. Here too, recalling his ancestor, Thomas, the poet, he tried his own hand at a poem for her:

> The grass shall cease to grow,
> The river's stream to run,
> The stars shall ponder in their course,
> No more shall shine the sun;
> The moon shall never wane or grow,
> The tide shall cease to ebb and flow,
> Ere I shall cease to love you.

Secrecy remained a priority. Once, as they returned from a trip to Pevensey, a crowd of young men recognised Parnell and shouted his name. The couple thought that they would escape detection by devising a plan to have a notice in the papers say that he was staying at Hastings with his sister, and had visited Pevensey.

When they travelled down by train from London, one would get out at Polegate where a carriage would be waiting to continue the journey, while the other would stay on the train as far as Eastbourne.

# 10

When Katharine returned occasionally to Eltham to check on Aunt Ben, Parnell would join her. Most times he took a cab but, on 21 May 1886, he was collected by Richard Wise (step-father of Thomas Partridge, the groom), a coachman employed at Wonersh Lodge. It was after midnight when the cab ran into a van from Sidcup.

The *Pall Mall Gazette* of 24 May reported the incident, under the heading, 'Mr. Parnell's Suburban Retreat':

> Shortly after midnight on Friday evening, Mr. Parnell, while driving home, came into collision with a market gardener's cart. During the sitting of Parliament the hon. member for Cork usually takes up his residence at Eltham, a suburban village in the south-east of London. From here he can often be seen taking riding exercise round by Chislehurst and Sidcup. On Friday night as usual his carriage met him at the railway station by the train which leaves Charing-cross at 11.45. As he was driving homeward a heavy van was returning from Covent-garden market, and this came into collision with Mr. Parnell's conveyance, damaging it, but fortunately causing no serious injury to its owner, who after a short pause continued his journey.

When Willie got to hear of this, he immediately sent a telegram to his wife, demanding an explanation. In her reply she called him by a pet name that she had given him so many years previously:

> My Boysie,
>
> I received your letter and, as I telegraphed, I have not the slightest idea of what it means unless it is meant to take a rise out of you ... I am inclined to think that Charlie [her brother, Charles Wood] is right. It is better to put up with a good deal of abuse rather than to retaliate. I should say the paragraph has been made up by Healy and Co. to annoy you. I should advise you to hold on to your seat.

Yours Truly,

K.

She then contacted Parnell, who wrote:

My dear Mrs. O'Shea,

Your telegram in reference to the paragraph duly reached me. I am very sorry that you should have any annoyance about the matter. I hope to see you on Sunday.

C.S. Parnell.

Willie was not very happy with their attempt to persuade him that it was a newspaper mistake, and he told Katharine to contact her uncle, Sir Evelyn Wood, or her brother, Charles Wood, presumably to take an action against the papers. This she refused to do.

F.S.L. Lyons points out that up to this date Katharine and Willie exchanged letters using their pet names, 'My Dick' and 'Boysie', and that prior to the Galway election Willie 'frequently complained to her of Parnell, as a man might write who expected a sympathetic hearing from the wife of his bosom'. It was Willie too, rather than Katharine, who initiated many invitations to Parnell to come to Eltham — but never after May 1886.

The Home Rule Bill, on which Parnell's political career hinged, was opposed by a dissenting Liberal, Lord Harrington. When Harrington's motion for its rejection was debated on 7 June 1886, Parnell made an eloquent appeal for its acceptance but it was defeated by 343 votes to 313, resulting in the dissolution of parliament and a second election within six months.

Willie's behaviour in this vote is worthy of note. Timothy Harrington later wrote:

Mr. Parnell, during the Galway election in 1886 explained to his followers that he had only adopted Captain O'Shea as

> candidate for Galway at the special request of Mr. Chamber-
> lain ... The strongest confirmation was given to it immediately
> after the election, when Captain O'Shea followed Mr. Cham-
> berlain out of the house of Commons, and refused to vote on
> the Home Rule Bill.

Again at a later date, Willie wrote to the Primate:

> If I were such a man ... who would buy a seat in Parliament at
> the price of his honour — I need only have given a silent vote
> for Mr. Gladstone's Home Rule Bill and my seat was as safe as
> any in Ireland.

When all the results were in, Gladstone had lost and his Liberal Party been weakened, the Conservatives were in power
(and would remain there for the following twenty years),
and Lord Salisbury was the new Prime Minister. Parnell
could no longer, as he had done in the recent past, offer his
votes to the highest bidder, and there was no Home Rule.
Irish politics were divided between the Home Rulers and the
Unionists.

Parnell tried vainly to seek release with Katharine from
his political tensions. On 31 July, Earnest Vinall, a house
agent, had a letter inquiring about rented accommodation
and stables at Moira House, in Eastbourne. The letter was
signed H. Campbell, but the writing was Katharine's. On 9
August, the agreement was sent to Palace Chambers, Westminster, for completion. Katharine and an unidentified
gentleman arrived to give final instructions — she chose the
wallpaper for the rooms and asked that five foot high lattice-
work be put around the top of the garden to give greater
privacy. A year's rent of £150 (£9,450) was paid in advance.
Mr Vinall had seen the same gentleman with Katharine at St.
John's Road.

Willie's behaviour was not helpful. He wrote to Katharine
suggesting that they move from Eltham, and received a
crushing reply, dated 25 August 1886:

> My Aunt says she will not give one penny to me either for the
> support of the children, or of course for yours either. She also
> says she understood that she was asked to buy the lease and
> furniture and pay the rent of your rooms at Albert Mansion ...
> If you mean to take a house for us away from Eltham let me
> know ... Of course in that case you will provide all monies for
> the children and myself.

Willie's utter financial dependence on Aunt Ben put an end
to that suggestion, but, as Aunt Ben was ninety-three years
old, it was generally felt that she could not last much longer.

Soon after the election, Parnell introduced a Land Bill into
the House of Commons. As prices had fallen, he proposed
no legal action be taken against tenants who were able to
pay half the rent plus arrears and other benefits. It was rejected on 21 September by 297 votes to 202, and Parnell
warned of a return to agrarian outrages.

Within a short time, he became very ill, and Katharine's
nursing was not successful. She took a house in London so
that he would not have to travel after the parliamentary
meetings, but he could not bear to be on his own and, a few
nights later, she heard a cab drive up and he was back in
Wonersh Lodge. Parnell became even more weak and nervous, so Katharine made an appointment for him, under the
name of Mr Stewart, with a well-known doctor, Sir Henry
Thompson. It was discovered that, among other things, he
had very poor circulation and that when his feet got cold, it
affected his stomach, which in turn affected his digestion.
Thereafter, Katharine made him keep a change of shoes and
socks in a little black bag which he carried around with him,
the contents of which bag caused much speculation among
his fellow MPs.

While Parnell was ill, he was visited at Eltham by William
O'Brien, to talk over ideas for a Plan of Campaign that was
being hatched. Parnell left the sick room for the first time to
receive O'Brien in the sitting room, but was soon exhausted.
On 23 October, *United Ireland* published an article, by Tim-

othy Harrington, about the plan, in which it was suggested that all estate tenants should band together to ask for a collective agreement for rent reduction. If this request were refused, they should pay nothing but should put the proposed reduced rent in a fund for evicted tenants which would be supplemented by the National League. Again the policy of boycotting would be introduced for farms of evicted tenants. Parnell did not agree but was too ill to resist it.

Ill-health made him more than ever dependent on Katharine. She would meet him at the House of Commons and the two would go out for a meal together, as he did not like the food at Westminster, and she was better able to keep him on his prescribed diet. He hated now the long journey home to Eltham on his own, and Katharine would often meet him at various railway stations, to break his journey.

Willie was away in Carlsbad at the time and, in October, a paragraph appeared in the *Sussex Daily News*, stating that when Katharine and Parnell had been in Eastbourne, Willie had known about it. Again Willie demanded an explanation, and Katharine calmly wrote:

> I know nothing about Mr. Parnell's movements in reference to Eastbourne, and I do not see how I should be expected to ... I do not regard the paragraph as one of importance but only as an attempt to draw you.

And Willie replied on 10 October:

> I am sorry you did not consult your solicitor because I think he would have advised you, in the interest of your children not to communicate with Mr Parnell.

Newspaper gossip reports were quite frequent and, on 18 December 1886, Gerard was with his father on the way to the Jem Mace benefit at the Cannon Street Hotel when another such article caught Willie's eye. He asked young Gerard if there was any truth in the rumours that Parnell was constantly at Eltham, and the boy, to protect his mother, said that it was not so. Having told the lie, he felt guilty and told his mother that he thought she was treating his father badly. This produced an 'immediate result' — or so Gerard thought. In fact, Katharine and Parnell once more went house hunting.

On the political front, the Plan of Campaign was gaining support. In Portumna, in Co. Galway, four hundred tenants marched to the offices of the agent of the Earl of Clanricarde, to demand a forty per cent reduction in the rents. The Earl had previously evicted tenants from Woodford. The request was refused and the tenants gave their rent money to William O'Brien and his followers. In December, Parnell, worried at the spread of the Plan, asked O'Brien to call a halt. He was afraid of losing the support of the Liberals. The Conservatives remained firmly against Home Rule.

Early in 1887, Arthur Balfour, a nephew of Prime Minister Salisbury, was appointed Chief Secretary for Ireland. His stated policy was:

> I shall be as relentless as Cromwell in enforcing obedience to the law, but, at the same time, I shall be as radical as any reformer in redressing grievances and especially in removing every cause of complaint in regard to the land.

# 11

Parnell used so many aliases that he became a little confused, and in January 1887, a farcical incident occurred. Mr George Porter, an auctioneer, was told that a Mr Fox had left a message that he was looking for a house. When Parnell called, he was taken for a walk to see St. John's Lodge at Tressilian Road in Brookley. Mr Porter said, 'This is a house that might interest you, it belongs to a Mr. Preston'. Without thinking, Parnell commented, 'Oh that's my name', which puzzled Mr Porter into saying, 'Why, I thought your name was Fox'. Parnell had to think quickly. 'No,' he said, 'that is the name of the friend I have been living with'. When asked for references, Parnell said that a man with horses should not be asked for references! Porter eventually agreed to a letting when £50 (£3,150) — half the rent — was produced.

Using the name Clement Preston, Parnell engaged a man called Honey as coachman. Honey's wife, Susan, was engaged by Katharine (introduced as Parnell's sister) for the position of housekeeper. The Honeys were employed for five months but, as Parnell was recognised and people gathered to see the famous man, he and Katharine decided to leave.

In March 1887, Katharine once more approached an estate agent — this time Hedges and Co., whose Mr Yates suggested they take a comfortable and pretty house at 34 York Terrace, which had a lovely view over Regent's Park. It was taken, for a period of two years, in the names of Mr and Mrs O'Shea. At first, Katharine suggested as a reference a certain Mr Preston, but this was not satisfactory, whereas Charles Stewart Parnell and the National Bank were acceptable enough.

Two servants were employed who adored Parnell — one was Esther Harvey, a parlour maid. Katharine left Parnell with a few works of Dickens and some technical books of an engineering nature, yet he begged not to be left alone. As was his custom when they were parted, each evening he sent her a telegram saying 'good night'.

Three weeks later, having left her aging aunt, Katharine sat up late, unable to read, thinking of Parnell and willing him to come to her. The clock struck two, then three, then, out of the dark night she heard the clip clop of a horse along the common, then by High Street, and into her road, coming to a halt outside:

> I knew now, and opened the door quickly as my lover came up the little side-walk past the window, giving the familiar signal as he went up the two steps; and I was in his arms as he whispered, 'Oh, my love, you must not leave me alone again.'

On 7 March 1887, *The Times* started a series of articles under the heading, 'Parnell and Crime', which stated that he and his followers '... have been, and are, in notorious and continuous relations with avowed murderers'. Parnell, well used to adverse newspaper reports, took no notice.

Concluding the articles on 18 April, *The Times* confided:

> ... besides the damning facts which we ... recorded, unpublished evidence existed which would bind still closer the links between the 'constitutional' chiefs and the contrivers of murder and outrage ... we do not think it right to withhold any longer from public knowledge the fact that we possess and have had in custody for some time documentary evidence which has a most serious bearing on the Parnellite conspiracy, and which, after a most careful and minute scrutiny, is, we are satisfied, quite authentic. We reproduce one document in facsimile to-day by a process the accuracy of which cannot be impugned, and we invite Mr. Parnell to explain how his signature has become attached to such a letter.

The published facsimile letter, was dated 15 May 1882— nine days after the Phoenix Park murders:

> Dear Sir,
>
> I am not surprised at your friend's anger but he and you should know that to denounce the murders was the only

course open to us. To do that promptly was plainly our best policy. But you can tell him and all others concerned that though I regret the accident of Lord F. Cavendish's death I cannot refuse to admit that Burke got no more than his desserts. You are at liberty to show him this, and others whom you can trust also, but let not my address be known. He can write to the House of Commons.

Yours very truly,

Chas. S. Parnell

The body of the letter was not, it was claimed, in Parnell's writing. However, the 'yours very truly' and the signature, 'unquestionably are so'. Furthermore:

> The body of the letter occupies the whole of the first page of an ordinary sheet of stout white notepaper, leaving no room in the same page for the signature, which is placed on the fourth page near the top right-hand corner. It was an obvious precaution to sign upon the back instead of upon the second page, so that the half-sheet might if necessary be torn off, and the letter disclaimed.

There are varying accounts of Parnell's reaction. Katharine said that some unknown person cut out the letters and pasted them on their gate. Without mentioning this to Parnell, she propped the paper against his breakfast teapot and he read it as he was eating his toast. She says that he went calmly to finish his assaying (He was trying to get enough gold from pieces of quartz taken from the stream near Avondale to make a wedding ring for her, but got only enough to line the ring), commenting only, 'Wouldn't you hide your head with shame if your King were so stupid as that, my Queen?'

R. Barry O'Brien writes that Parnell on going to the House of Commons that evening was shown the paper by Harrington, who expected a denial. Parnell merely said, 'I did not make an S. like that since 1878', and Harrington's immediate thought was '… if this is the way he is going to deal with the

15/5/82

Dear Sir,

I am not surprised at your friends anger but I and you should know that to denounce the murders was the only course open to us. To do that promptly was plainly our best policy.

But you can tell him and all others concerned that though I regret the accident of Lord F Cavendish's death I cannot refuse to admit that Burke got no more than his deserts

You are at liberty to show him, and others whom you can trust also, but let not my letters be known. You can write to House of Commons

Yours very truly
Chas. S. Parnell

letter in the House, there is not an Englishman who will not believe that he wrote it'.

It was 1 o'clock in the morning before Parnell had the opportunity of denouncing the letter in Parliament. He said:

> ... when I saw what purported to be my signature, I saw plainly that it was an audacious and unblushing fabrication. Why sir, many members of this House have seen my signature, and if they will compare it with what purports to be my signature in the 'Times' of this morning they will see there are only two letters in the whole name which bear any resemblance to letters in my own signature as I write it. I cannot understand how the managers of a responsible and what used to be a respectable journal could have been so hoodwinked, so hoaxed, so bamboozled....

Many expected Parnell to take an action against *The Times* immediately. John Morley writes:

> Now and afterwards people asked why Mr. Parnell did not promptly bring his libellers before a court of law. The answer was simple. The case would naturally have been tried in London, in other words, not only the plaintiff's own character, but the whole movement that he represented, would have been submitted to a Middlesex jury, with all the national and political prejudices inevitable in such a body, and with all the twelve chances of a disagreement, that would be almost as disastrous to Mr. Parnell as an actual verdict for his assailants. The issues were too great to be exposed to the hazards of a cast of the die....

Had Parnell been acquitted in Dublin it would have been discounted in England. Parnell departed for Ireland, giving the excuse that he was ill. Early in May, the government refused Gladstone's request for a select committee. On Parnell's return to the House in mid-May, a fellow MP commented, 'If ever death shone in a face it shone in that one. It was the first indication that he was suffering from Bright's disease, to those who understood illness'. Others blamed his hectic life. T.P. O'Connor wrote:

> ... in the course of a couple of years, Parnell, bright, alert, thin, distinguished, with triumphant youth in every look, drifted into a sickly-looking sluggish, middle-aged man, dressed in the clothes of a valetudinarian shopkeeper.

Although she does not mention this time, Katharine must have been alarmed and probably nursed him at Eltham, and Gerard would have told his father of this. Willie later said to Chamberlain that it was in June 1887 that he first suspected there was any truth in the rumours. Through Gerard, Willie contacted his wife on 13 June, threatening an action if she did not break with Parnell. On 27 June 1887, she wrote to her son:

> My dear Gerardie,
>
> I now write to confirm my telegram to you in which I said I was willing to meet the wishes you expressed in regard to Mr. Parnell. I am most anxious everything should be made as pleasant as possible for you, and that nobody should come here who is in any way obnoxious to you, and I therefore readily agree that there shall be no further communication direct or indirect with him.
>
> Ever, my darling Gerardie,
>
> Your loving Mother.

The following day she wrote again to her son, saying she would give up the stables and that she was not afraid of any proceedings.

It seems reasonable to believe Willie's statement that he did not suspect his wife until June 1887 — the letters and the constant house moves would seem to confirm this. There was, however, an incident that Katharine did not include in her book but later told Henry Harrison, to imply that Willie knew and was a party to the affair. She said that on one occasion Willie and Parnell were both at Eltham to discuss some important political matter, so she went to bed early. Willie, who was the next to retire, saw her door open, stopped to talk to her, and the door closed. Katharine continued:

> Suddenly, the door was banged violently open and Mr. Parnell
> stalked in, his head held high and his eyes snapping; he said
> not a word but marched straight up to me, picked me up,
> threw me over his shoulder and turned on his heel; still with-
> out a word, he marched out of the room across the landing and
> into his own room, where he threw me down on the bed and
> shut the door ... I do not think that Captain O'Shea was left in
> doubt as to Mr. Parnell's attitude....

She did not give a date for this event but, as she was in her
mid-thirties when she met Parnell, and was pregnant for a
large part of the first three years of their affair, she would
have it believed that it happened after 1886, when she was in
her forties and a mother of six children, by which time Parnell would have been weak from illness.

If Willie was a party to the deception, why did he challenge Parnell to the duel? Why, when articles appeared in
the paper, did he contact Katharine to ask their meaning?
Why, if Willie knew about it, did she write so many letters of
assurance that there was nothing to the affair? Surely, at
least, he would not have questioned his son as to Parnell's
movements, and would not have sent messages by him.

In an interview in the *Freeman's Journal* on 30 December
1889, just after Willie filed for divorce, Parnell was quoted as
saying that:

> Capt. O'Shea was always aware that he was constantly there
> [Eltham] in his absence from 1880 to 1886 and since 1886 he
> had known that Mr. Parnell constantly resided there from 1880
> to 1886.

Conor Cruise O'Brien refers to this statement as '... carrying
a fairly clear implication that Parnell, over a period of years
— 1880–86 — had been living with Mrs O'Shea in her husband's absence and without his knowledge at the time'.
Again, Willie's claim, that he did not know until 1887,
could have been true, He had to accept assurances given to

Gerard during the summer of 1886, as there was little he could do until Aunt Ben died and their finances were resolved.

It was suggested that the constant house moves were to throw the press off the scent of the affair, but again, if Willie were part of the conspiracy it would be far easier to stay at Wonersh Lodge — less noticeable for the papers at least. Some facts are indisputable — Katharine and Willie, although their marriage still survived, were no longer in love when she met Parnell; Parnell and Katharine's love was instant and lasted until he died; he would have married her immediately if she had been free; and he considered her his wife. Money certainly dictated the unhappy situation that ensued, and the need to protect her children also played a large part. Certain aspects were never clarified — how much Willie knew; when he knew it; and whether, to cover her affair with Parnell, Katharine, by giving him occasional conjugal rights, gave him reason to believe that the last three children were his.

However much or little Willie knew, Katharine's letter to Gerard in June 1887 intimated that Parnell would no longer stay at the house. He may have gone to stay at York Terrace for a while or to the house — at Walsingham Terrace, Brighton — that she later admitted to having taken in 1887. By August of that year, he was writing to her from Avondale: '...whenever you are ready for me I can return'. In writing of this period, she tells, instead, of their discussion on whether or not he should bring an action against *The Times* in regard to the forged letter.

The *Times* letter was used for political ends by Salisbury, who taunted the Liberals for consorting with a man who condoned assassination. This helped the passing of the Criminal Law Amendment Bill, despite Parnell's obstruction. The Bill became law in mid-July. It did not have to be renewed by parliament every few years and was a help to Balfour, as certain organisations could be suppressed and districts where disturbances were taking place could be 'proclaimed'. In these proclaimed areas, people who took part in boycotting or resistance to eviction could be tried without a jury. Many Plan of Campaign supporters were jailed, including 24 MPs, and Balfour insisted that all prisoners — whether political or not — should be treated in the same way. Soon after the Criminal Law Amendment Bill, a Land Act was also passed to help balance it. 100,000 lease holders could go to the Land Court; the county courts could grant stays of eviction; and Parnell's amendment was accepted, enabling judicial rents to be revised after three years. This, at least, was welcome.

However, Parnell still wanted Home Rule by constitutional means, and, to show solidarity with Gladstone and to appeal to his own people for restraint, he attended a banquet at the National Liberal Club in July 1887.

In September 1887, William O'Brien and a local farmer, John Mandeville, were to be tried, at Mitchelstown, Co. Cork, under the new Criminal Law Amendment Bill. The Irish National League called a protest meeting in the market square and the magistrate in charge could not get through. The police, greatly outnumbered by the protesters, panicked and opened fire. Three men were killed and others wounded. Balfour privately opposed but publicly had to support the police action. The Liberals and the Irish party were once more united. In prison, William O'Brien and others refused to wear prison clothes and were roughly treated. Shortly after his release, John Mandeville died and the government was blamed.

Although sorely missed by the Irish party, Parnell disappeared from public view once more. His health was not good and he spent some time in England with Katharine and some in Avondale. He was traced to the address in Brockley by a detective employed by *The Times*. On 26 November 1887, the paper published an article stating:

> With reference to the mystery which has attached to Mr. Parnell's recent movements, we are enabled to inform the public,

as the result of inquiries on the spot, that the leader of the Irish Nationalist Party has been living, under the name of Mr. C. Preston, at 112 Tressilian Road, Brockley, a house which he took in the name of Preston about a year ago. He has received letters there under the same name. Mr. Parnell has been at Brockley within the last fortnight.

In an attempt to avoid publicity, Parnell, early in the new year, went back once more to Avondale. His sister, Emily Dickenson, was there at the time and his mother Delia had used for dancing and theatricals his new cattle shed (modelled on the new station at Brighton that Parnell had studied). This entertainment would go on until six in the morning. Parnell insisted that the shed should be returned to its rightful tenants — the cattle!

The Plan of Campaign, not completely crushed, was supported by some members of the Catholic Church, including Archbishop Croke of Cashel and Archbishop Walsh of Dublin. Balfour, Salisbury and some English clergy sent protests to Rome, and on 20 April 1888, a Papal Rescript was issued condemning the Plan. Some of the Irish leaders got around this by saying that the Rescript was based on a misunderstanding of the true position in Ireland. On 8 May, Parnell spoke at a meeting of the English Liberals and pointed out that he had never approved of the Plan which had been conceived when he was ill, that the Rescript was politically irrelevant (thus pointing out that Home Rule was not Rome rule), and urging his fellow countrymen to bear in mind the alliance with the English Liberals. In giving his own views, in advance of a meeting called for 17 May 1888, for Catholic members, Parnell was emphasising the fact that he was still the leader.

While the Irish leaders, O'Brien and Dillon, were disturbed by Parnell's anti-Plan speech, the meeting on 17 May also took the view that Rome could not interfere in the political life of Ireland. A resolution was passed by the Catholic MPs:

We, as guardians, in common with our brother representatives of other creeds, of those civil liberties which our Catholic forefathers have resolutely defended, feel bound solemnly to reassert that Irish Catholics can recognise no right in the Holy See to interfere with the Irish people in the management of their political affairs.

The Plan continued, but the rift widened between on the one side, O'Brien and Dillon, and on the other, their leader, who preferred to pursue Home Rule rather than agrarian conflict.

# 12

Katharine's story — that she and Parnell discussed the *Times* letter — was, undoubtedly, true. Parnell also discussed the letter with many of his followers. When the question of a libel case was suggested, some thought that a special commission at parliament level would be more appropriate than a case against *The Times*.

Meanwhile, *The Times* continued with its series of articles, one of which caused an ex-MP, Mr Frank Hugh O'Donnell, to take an action against the paper. Parnell went with O'Donnell to inspect the letters he was supposed to have written. These included one with two mis-spellings, supposedly written on 9 January 1882 to Patrick Egan:

> Dear E.,
>
> What are these people waiting for? This inaction is inexcuseable. Our best men are in prison and nothing is being done. Let there be an end to this hesitency. Prompt action is called for. You undertook to make it hot for old Foster and Co. Let us have some evidence of your power to do so. My health is good, thanks.
>
> Yours very truly,
>
> Chas. S. Parnell.

With the collapse of O'Donnell's action, which came to court in July 1888, counsel for *The Times*, Attorney General Sir Richard Webster gave a long-winded summation which went over all the statements made against Parnell in *The Times*. These could not remain unchallenged. Parnell, in frigid tones, made a statement in the House of Commons denouncing the letters as forgeries: 'The great majority of them are palpable forgeries — most undoubted forgeries; they bear the look of forgery on their very face'. Of the letter to Egan, dated 9 January 1882, he said: 'I never wrote it; I never signed it; I never directed it to be written; I never authorised it to be written and I never saw it.'

Again the choice was between a court case and government commission. On 16 July 1888, W.H. Smith moved the introduction of the Members of Parliament Bill which became known as the Special Commission Bill. The parameters of this were debated, as some felt that it held too wide a brief. Parnell felt that it would include a whole investigation into the Land League. Chamberlain cleverly said that, although he had formed a very good opinion of Parnell, this would be changed only if he refused a full enquiry. Parnell retaliated that a full enquiry would produce more unpleasant facts about Chamberlain. In this row, Willie O'Shea sided with Chamberlain. However, Chamberlain eventually realised that Willie had carried incorrect information between himself and Parnell in 1885. After several exchanges of letters in *The Times*, Chamberlain had to back down:

> ... neither at this time nor subsequently has it appeared to me that there was anything in these communications of which Mr. Parnell had cause to be ashamed.

Gladstone felt that the commission was better than none at all. Slowly, the bill moved through committee with nominal protests. Tim Healy offered his services to join in Parnell's defence. According to R. Barry O'Brien, it was not Parnell's decision to reject Healy's offer — he consented at once but Davitt was the one who objected. An old Fenian said at the time: 'Healy seems to have the best political head of all these people', to which Parnell replied, 'He has the only political head among them'. Healy, however, blamed Parnell, and was quite bitter about having been rejected.

Katharine had discussed Parnell's position with two legal luminaries, George Lewis and Sir Charles Russell. An incident which amused both Parnell and herself occurred when Lewis asked him to call before the case. Lewis and Sir

Charles, while hoping that Parnell would not be annoyed, said that they were worried about his clothes (shades of T.P. O'Connor's 'clothes of a valetudinarian shopkeeper'!), and suggested that he invest in a new frock-coat from Poole's. When it was finished, he and Katharine had fun trying it on in front of her long mirror, 'Parnell stroking its silk facings with pride'. Mr Lewis, who was a dapper dresser, confided in Katharine that he found Parnell's Irish homespuns 'a great trial', and she, repressing laughter, replied that she thought it wonderful that he was above clothes!

On 17 September 1888, Messrs Hannen, Day and Smith began work on the commission which did not end until 22 November 1889. In his book, *The Life of Gladstone*, John Morley writes that the 'proceedings speedily settled down into the most wearisome drone that was ever heard in a court of law'. However, he gives a vivid description of some of the witnesses:

> There was the peasant from Kerry in his frieze swallow-tail and kneebreeches, and the woman in her scarlet petticoat who runs barefoot over the bog in Galway. The convicted member of a murder club was brought up in custody from Mountjoy Prison or Maryborough ... One of the most popular of the Irish representatives had been fetched from his dungeon, and was to be seen wandering through the lobbies in search of his warders ... Witnesses were produced in a series that seemed interminable to tell the story of five-and-twenty outrages in Mayo, of as many in Cork, of forty-two in Galway, of sixty-five in Kerry, one after another, and all with immeasurable detail. Some of the witnesses spoke no English, and the English of others was hardly more intelligible than Erse. Long extracts were read out from four hundred and forty speeches ... The three judges groaned.

St. John Ervine describes another of the 450 witnesses:

> Delaney, one of the Phoenix Park murderers, a middle-aged-sized, stoutish man, with yellow-red hair, looking more like a Russian than an Irishman, who gave evidence in favour of the *Times*.

It was not until 14 February 1889, the fiftieth day of the commission, that the matter of the letters was raised. The Parnellites had carried out their own investigations long before this. At first, Parnell had suspected that Willie had a hand in the matter. However, in August 1888, Patrick Egan, to whom the second letter was supposedly addressed, was contacted and gave concrete evidence of the real forger. Egan, who was in Lincoln, Nebraska at the time, remembered back to 1881 — when he had acted in negotiations with Richard Pigott, who was selling his newspapers to Parnell — and compared letters from Pigott, dated 1881, with the facsimile letters published by *The Times*. Not alone was the writing similar, but some phrases were the same, and the word 'hesitancy' had been misspelt as 'hesitency'. He wrote at once that Pigott was the forger.

Pigott was in Ireland in September 1888 and was sent a message that an American wanted to meet him in London on important business. He arrived on 24 October, and at first denied to Parnell that he had any knowledge of the letters, but later confessed to Lewis, his solicitor, and promised to give a written confession the next day. Detectives followed Pigott and said that he met representatives from *The Times*. Pigott decided to brazen it out and the confession was not made. If confronted, he would say that Parnell and friends had offered him £1,000 (£63,000) to say that he had forged the letters!

Just one week later, on 31 October 1888, the third witness for *The Times* was called — Willie O' Shea. Parnell took his seat very early. Up to a week previously, he had been so sure that Willie had some hand in the forged letters that Pigott's confession had not completely put his mind at rest, and he wanted to hear for himself what Willie had to say. While the Dublin *Daily Express* of 2 November said of Willie: 'If possible he was a greater dandy than ever', and commented on the 'fresh cluster of curls about his ears' and the gold eyeglasses he used 'with an eighteenth-century grace', others did not share this view — St. John Ervine said that his look had entirely altered: even the colour of his face, moustache and whiskers had changed and prematurely aged. Certainly he was nervous.

His evidence concerned the Kilmainham Treaty and his part in it. He spoke of the time he had carried messages to and from Chamberlain. When asked if he were on friendly terms with Parnell while they were both Members of Parliament he replied, 'Yes'. He went on to say that he wanted to clear his name in regard to the letters, as Chamberlain had told him that Parnell suspected he was involved in at least procuring the facsimile letter. He became very nervous when questioned about the letters, wiping his face, clasping his head in his hands, twisting and turning his hands and keeping his eyes fixed on the floor. He said that he thought Parnell was innocent of outrage, but added the words: 'even after I changed my opinion of Mr. Parnell'. When asked to clarify this statement, he replied, with reference to 1886, that '... certain things came to my knowledge at that time which absolutely destroyed the good opinion I had hitherto held of Mr. Parnell'. He was not pressed further on this. At first he said he did not think the letter in *The Times* was genuine, although he thought the writing was genuine. His evidence added little to the case.

According to J.L. Garvin, having given evidence, the unhappy Willie wrote to Chamberlain in November 1888:

> As I am going away I had better tell you that the anxiety I felt was occasioned by the fact that Mrs. O'Shea is under a written engagement not to communicate directly or indirectly with Mr. Parnell, and the latter under a written order not to do so with Mrs. O'Shea. I daresay a great many people have some notion of the state of affairs, but I am most anxious for my children's sake that nothing about it should be actually published, because a very large fortune for them may depend upon it not coming into print. I believe Mrs. Wood of Eltham is worth £200,000 [£12,600,000] or more, all left to them, and ... Mrs. O'Shea's relations would use any weapon to change her will. Years ago I begged that affairs should be so arranged that in no case could I myself inherit any of this money. It is on their

account that I can safely say to you that the anxiety was in no way personal.

Shortly after this, Willie left for Spain where he had business concerns.

# 13

On the fiftieth day of the hearing, 14 February 1889, the manager of *The Times* was called to give evidence. He said he was convinced from the start that the letters were genuine. When he was asked why he came to this conclusion, he said that he felt they were just the sort of letters Parnell would write, and felt that the public would be of this opinion also. He said that he did not ask from where the letters came!

It was not until 2.40 p.m. on 20 February that Richard Pigott eventually took the oath in the witness box. He was slightly late as he had been having lunch at the Duval Restaurant across the street, and the public rose to get a better view of this unimpressive looking man. The newspapers agreed that he was was bald, bearded, small and stout. He was asked if he knew of the charges to be made against Parnell, and he replied that he had no knowledge of them until the first articles appeared in *The Times*. This was contradicted immediately and he was very surprised to hear being read a letter he had written, on 4 March 1887 — just before the publication of the first article on Parnellism and Crime — to Dr Walsh, Archbishop of Dublin, saying that the Parnellite party was about to be destroyed and that he had proof of the truth of what would be said. This was followed by two more letters — one to Mr Foster begging for a reward for his good services to the Crown, and the second to the Land League, through Patrick Egan, asking for money for his services to nationalism. The public laughed at the tone of the letters, and Pigott's complaint that it was not amusing only increased the laughter.

On Friday 22 February, the cross-examination continued. During the afternoon, Sir Charles Russell explained that he had asked Pigott to write a number of words the day before, including the word 'hesitancy' which Pigott had misspelt with an 'e'. At this point, the case was adjourned. Parnell warned his solicitor that Pigott would not appear again in court, that he might flee the country if not watched. This is exactly what happened.

Mr Henry Labouchere, of 24 Grosvenor Gardens, had an unexpected visitor on Saturday, 23 February 1889. A supporter of the Irish party, he had been involved in trying to get a confession from Pigott on his visit to London the previous October, and was surprised to see him on his doorstep again. Pigott said that he was willing to put his confession in writing. Labouchere asked his servant to call in their neighbour, George Augustus Sala, a newspaper man. Sala, who was to act as witness, noted that, while Pigott was outwardly cool, his hand shook as he wrote the full confession. Having signed it, he took himself off to the Alhambra Music Hall.

Pigott's housekeeper was paid off the following Monday with £5 (£315), and was instructed to burn all the papers Pigott left behind in a black box. This she did and could not tell what they contained. That night at 11 o'clock, he slipped past the police guard at Anderson's Hotel in Fleet Street, and by Tuesday morning, when the court resumed, he was in Paris.

The court was crowded on that Tuesday morning, 26 February 1889, when an usher called for Richard Pigott and no one appeared. It took some time for the fact to register that he had taken off and was not available for the remainder of the case. Sir Charles immediately looked for and got a warrant for his arrest. Parnell went to Scotland Yard to see if they had any idea of the whereabouts of Pigott, but to no avail. There he left behind his mysterious black bag, the one that contained the change of shoes and socks that Katharine insisted he carry with him. It amused him to think of the faces of the Scotland Yard detectives when they opened the bag!

The following morning, Pigott's confession, posted in Paris, was handed to the Secretary of the Commission. A section of it reads as follows:

> The circumstances with the obtaining of the letters, as I gave in evidence, are not true. No one, save myself, was concerned in the transaction. I told Mr. Houston [of *The Times*] that I had discovered the letters in Paris, but I grieve to have to confess that I simply fabricated them, using genuine letters of Messrs. Parnell and Egan in copying certain words, phrases, and general character of the handwriting. I traced some words and phrases by putting the genuine letters against the window and placing the sheets on which I wrote over it. These genuine letters were the letters from Mr. Parnell, copies of which have been read in court, and four or five letters from Mr. Egan which were also read in court. I destroyed these letters after using them. Some of the signatures I traced in this manner and some I wrote. I then wrote to Houston, telling him to come to Paris for the documents. I told him that they had been placed in a black bag with some old accounts, scraps of paper, and old newspapers. On his arrival I produced to him the letters, accounts, and scraps of paper. After a very brief inspection he handed me a cheque on Cook for £500 [£31,500] the price that I told him I had agreed to pay for them. At the same time he gave me £105 [£6,615] in bank-notes as my own commission.

When this confession was read in full, the Attorney General, on behalf of *The Times*, withdrew from consideration the question as to the authenticity of the letters. Parnell appeared in the witness box to deny formally that he had signed any of the documents. The Commission found the documents to be forgeries, and later that month *The Times* paid Parnell £5,000 (£315,000) as damages for libel.

There was a warrant out for Pigott's arrest. On 28 February, he had arrived in Madrid from Paris and had booked into the Embajadores Hotel in the name of Roland Ponsonby. He sent a telegram to Mr Shannon, his Irish solicitor, through the offices of Mr Soames of Lincoln's Inn Fields, to send 'what he promised'. He went out then to a picture gallery and, by remarkable chance, was seen by Willie O'Shea in a café.

When Soames received the telegram he contacted the police, who then knew the whereabouts of Pigott. Next morning, Pigott checked in his hotel to see if the expected money had arrived and was apprehensive when it had not. At 4.30 p.m. the police arrived at the hotel and were shown up to his first floor room. When Pigott saw the Inspector, he murmured something about his luggage. Before anyone could stop him, he grabbed a revolver, put it to his mouth and pulled the trigger. John Morley writes:

> They found on his corpse the scapulary worn by devout Catholics as a visible badge and token of allegiance to the heavenly powers. So in the ghastliest wreck of life, men still hope and seek for some mysterious cleansing of the soul that shall repair all.

In the House of Commons that night, Parnell received a standing ovation, led by Gladstone. The commission took another few days to finish, but for the public it was over. Parnell, who had been most unpopular, was now treated as a hero and cheered wherever he went. Immediately the result of the Commission was known, he was made a life member of the National Liberal Club. He made a speech once more in support of Ireland's demand for Home Rule, asking the Liberals to give this demand recognition, and his speech was widely reported in the newspapers. Parnell, the uncrowned King of Ireland, was at the height of his power. Over the years he had grown in stature, had united the Irish party and had frequently, in the British parliament, initiated discussions on the subject of Home Rule for Ireland.

A week later, he was honoured for the second time by the Liberals at the Eighty Club, and shook hands publicly with Lord Spencer, who had been the Lord Lieutenant at the time of the Phoenix Park murders. Again, a few days after this, he was given an ovation at a great meeting at the St. James' Club, and on 28 May, Sir Charles and Lady Russell gave a reception in his honour.

Parnell was not a man who sought acclaim, and he commented to Katharine that the only bright spot of the latter reception was meeting the Irish poet, Katharine Tynan. To all of this adulation he seemed indifferent. He had been educated in England and had spent much time there, but he felt more at home in Ireland. Katharine's account quotes him as saying: '… when I am in the midst of a peasant crowd in Ireland … I feel a little as I do when I see you smile across the street at me before we meet'.

She was very proud of him when large numbers of people gave him enthusiastic acclaim but he told her that he believed the English cheered him because he had been found to be within the law, a law that they worshipped. He warned her:

> Don't be too pleased with the clapping of these law lovers, Queenie. I have a presentiment that you will hear them another way before long, and I am exactly the same, either way!

# 14

Katharine says that, from 1888, Aunt Ben's health was failing, and that she would walk across to the house nearly every night to check on the old lady. Still the aunt lingered on into her ninety-seventh year and it was not until the morning of 19 May 1889 when Katharine was admitted by Aunt Ben's personal maid that the realisation dawned that the end was near. Katharine describes the scene:

> ... my aunt, who was breathing with difficulty, whispered as I bent down to kiss her hand, 'You do believe, do you not, my Swan?' I answered, 'Yes, Auntie, of course I do believe, most firmly.' She said, 'I am glad. I wish you could come with me, my darling!' and I sobbingly told her that I wished I could too. I stayed by her side and smoothed her hand till she ceased to breathe, and then waited by her as all her servants who had been with her for many years, filed past the bed, and took a last look at their stern but just and much-loved mistress.

Katharine felt that she could not stay on at Wonersh Lodge, and took the family to Nottingham, and then on to 10 Walsingham Terrace, Brighton — a house she had taken with Parnell in 1887:

> ... the position was attractive to us: cornfields from one side of the house away up to Shoreham basin and harbour, a waste of hay at the back of the house, an excellent train service and a sufficient distance from Brighton proper to enable us to avoid the crowd.

The house afforded magnificent views and they would marvel together at the wonderful sunsets over the harbour, and contrast the 'prosaic ugliness' of midday with the golden evenings.

No mention was made of the written agreement with Willie to stay apart from Parnell. He had a study of his own in the dining-room and a furnace in the basement for his assaying. The assaying was exceedingly hot and she would inveigle him to go for rides on President in the fresh air across the Downs. She would show the dogs his whip and cap and they would jump around until he relented and took them out.

She made no reference to the long-awaited will of Aunt Ben. Though not as large as was expected, the entire fortune of £145,000 (£9,135,000) in consols and land in Gloucestershire was left to Katharine, apart from a few minor legacies, and Harrison states that it could not be made the subject of any claim by her husband, nor brought within the operation of her marriage settlement. The will had been made in the last fifteen months of Aunt Ben's life and, according to F.S.L. Lyons, the Wood family had tried, in an attempt to invalidate it, to have the old woman certified as insane before her death, but Parnell and Katharine had written to Gladstone to have his physician, Sir Andrew Clark, certify otherwise.

The Wood family were joined by Willie in claiming that Katharine had used her position as companion to Aunt Ben to put undue pressure on the old lady to ensure that the estate came to her alone. This dispute delayed for three years the distribution of the legacies.

Willie's claims to Chamberlain that he had no personal interest were set aside — he wanted a share for himself as well as for his children. One way of succeeding with charges against Katharine would be to show that she had deceived him for a number of years. He saw more paragraphs in newspapers in September 1889, and consulted his solicitor. He knew that Katharine was staying in Brighton at this time and went down to a nearby hotel but saw her only at the theatre.

On 19 October, Willie wrote to Cardinal Manning, saying that he was going to file for divorce. The Cardinal asked on what grounds, and Willie produced the original article from the *Pall Mall Gazette*. The Cardinal took over a month to reply, and in that time he consulted with others. On 27 November, he wrote to say there was insufficient evidence, that Willie had waited a surprisingly long time before bringing charges, and he hinted that this delay might have been due to financial considerations. Willie, very annoyed, wrote back within twenty-four hours. More letters followed, and an interview. The last letter from the Cardinal was dated 17 December.

There was quite a domestic scene in Brighton when Gerard, realising that Parnell was again staying with his mother, seized Parnell's belongings and threw them out the window. Willie later said in evidence that having received information that Parnell was staying there on 20 December, he filed for divorce on Christmas Eve.

Between that December 1889 and the following November, when the case was heard, many options were considered by all parties. Parnell definitely wanted a divorce so that he could marry Katharine. She wanted to fight it on the grounds of Willie's infidelity. In her book she says of Willie, 'I knew absolutely nothing of his private life, and cared less', but she told Harrison that she knew of about seventeen such cases. She did not substantiate this apart from the amazing claim that he had committed adultery with Anna Steele, her own sister, in 1881, at a time when Anna was making the peace in Katharine's home by telling Willie that there was no truth in the stories about Parnell! Even Willie was taken by surprise at this accusation. F.S.L. Lyons says that, in a letter Willie wrote to Chamberlain in August 1890, '... though excessively self-righteous, [he] is vehement enough to carry some conviction'. Willie wrote that it was:

> ... absolutely unfounded ... that in 1881 I committed adultery with one of her sisters. During the intervening nine years she has not hinted such a thing either to myself or to any member of the family. You can imagine the indignation of her brothers and sisters. Low as she had sunk with him before, I confess I was astonished when I heard of the depths to which Parnell had now dragged her....

The accusation may have resulted from the fact that Anna had put in a claim for a share of Aunt Ben's money. An alternative explanation is that Willie's annoyance in that same year, 1881, when he thought Katharine was having him followed by a detective, may have been construed as implying that he had something to hide.

Katharine also wanted to fight the divorce on the grounds that Willie connived in the affair, but as this would have led to a collapse in the divorce proceedings, Parnell would not agree. Certainly Willie had known about the affair since 1886/7 but remained silent because of the financial position. Connivance would, however, be difficult to prove.

Would a divorce affect Parnell's political career? Katharine feared that it would while he seems not to have given this question much consideration. He knew that Gladstone held him in high regard and he had visited him at Hawarden as late as 18 December 1889. According to John Morley, Gladstone wrote in his own record:

> Reviewed and threw into form all the points of possible amendment or change in the plan of Irish Government, etc. for my meeting with Mr. Parnell. He arrived at 5.30, and we had two hours of satisfactory conversation; but he put off the gros of it.

Next day he continued:

> Two hours more with Mr. P. on points in Irish government plans. He is certainly one of the very best people to deal with that I have ever known. Took him to the old castle. He seems to notice and appreciate everything.

The Irish people too, Parnell felt would back him — had they not backed him twice against the urgings of the Catholic Church? He ignored the fact that adultery was an enormous crime in Ireland, believing that as long as he was needed politically, his private life would be sacrosanct. As early as 14 January 1890, he wrote to William O'Brien:

My dear O'Brien,

I thank you very much indeed for your kind letter, which I shall always highly prize. If this case is ever fully gone into (a matter which is exceedingly doubtful) you may rest assured that it will be shown that the dishonour and the discredit have not been on my side. I trust you will not allow anything to interfere with the certainty of your being able to be present at the opening of the Session. Believe me,

Yours very sincerely,

Chas. S. Parnell.

Parnell needed the support of his friends more than ever and must have taken to heart the death of Joseph Biggar that February, but he was in no way embarrassed by his equivocal position. He was present at the first night of the session of the House of Commons on 11 February 1890 for a motion in connection with the forged letter. He did not listen to the debate because, Morley says:

> He had a sincere contempt for speeches in themselves, and was wont to set down most of them to vanity. A message was sent that he should come upstairs and speak ... His speech was admirable; firm without emphasis, penetrating, dignified, freezing, and unanswerable. Neither now nor on any later occasion save one did his composure in public or in private give way.

An alternative open to Parnell and Katharine, or so they thought, was to pay Willie either to drop the case or to allow Katharine to divorce him — £20,000 (£1,260,000) was mentioned frequently as a suitable sum — but, because the family was disputing Aunt Ben's will, Katharine could not readily lay hands on that amount of money.

St. John Ervine puts Willie's position clearest:

> He had great talents, but he seems not to have had character. In suitable circumstances, he might have followed a career of considerable worth, but the circumstances were not created for

him. His climbing father had thrown him into extravagant company with instructions to be as extravagant as them all, and he had obeyed his father's instructions with a fidelity that appalled his parent ... and the disservice done to him by his father was not rectified by the snivelling piety of his mother ... It is conceivable that Captain O'Shea might never have achieved any more than he did, whatever his circumstances were, for a mean mind cannot be other than mean in any state. But we cannot deny that this unfortunate man suffered in an encounter which, however it ended, could not result in any happiness for him. Thousands of his countrymen regarded him as a complacent husband, ready to consent to his wife's adultery if it brought him a job, and he was maligned in print and in public speech as if he were the lowest of mankind. He does not command our respect, but neither does he deserve this condemnation. We may never know what agonies of mind he endured or what fierce resentments he nourished in his heart ... This was a man born to play a part which could not please anyone, himself least of all, and he played it in circumstances which bereft him of sympathy or compassion.

Willie was not quite bereft of sympathy as his son, Gerard, despite his mother's great love for him, and her constant assurances, stood by his father. Carmen too, the third child, eventually stayed with her father while Norah remained faithful to her mother until Katharine's death. In fact, the position of all the children was unenviable. All of them, including Parnell's two daughters, were reared with the name of O'Shea and were taken to church on Sundays by Willie, while living with Katharine and Parnell. They would all have been aware that Parnell was staying with their mother. This is glossed over in Katharine's account of the early months of 1890 spent in Brighton. She describes how:

Often in the following spring my King and I would drive out as far as the foot of the Downs near the training stables beyond Southwick; and then, climbing to the crest of the hills, go for long walks, away over the Downs ... As we walked along hand in hand we were gay in the glorious spring of the year, feeling that while love walked so closely with us youth could not lag too far behind, and in the wide expanse of the South Downs,

> which appealed so much to both our natures, we forgot all care
> and trouble.

Following this romantic outpouring, she gives details of
their very private lives spent so happily in Brighton during
the months of waiting for the court case. They would watch
a shepherd work his flock with his dog or horses on the
nearby training ground, galloping with a great joy of living.
A little shop in Pool Valley which sold various stones was
another favourite haunt, and here Parnell found some onyx
ball beads he had made into a chain, alternating two onyx
beads with one gold ball, and added a locket for her. When
the finished chain proved too heavy and rubbed against her
neck, he forbade her to wear it any more. In a second-hand
book shop in North Street he could indulge his interests in
mining or mechanics, while she would discuss with the pro-
prietor the poets 'of a bygone age'.

He would take a few days leave from Katharine to go to
his shooting lodge, Aughavanagh, near Avondale, where she
could not follow, and she would always ensure that he was
well provided with warm clothes and good food. She did
not like the 'stewed' tea made in the Irish fashion, and
taught him to make his own but, when he said that his
friends preferred his own special tea, she labelled that 'for
presents' and the less choice one 'For Mr. Parnell's own use',
thus fooling his companions into taking the less tasty
supply.

He had a creative mind and would give all his free time to
his latest invention. In Brighton at that time it was a design
for a ship that would be impervious to the motion of heavy
seas. This, he told her, would make their fortunes! He made
several models that were tried out at Chain Pier, Brighton.
When her children came on a few days visit, Parnell would
stay near the pier and they would join in the experiments.

The descriptions could be of a very happily married
couple, and it was as such that Parnell and Katharine considered themselves. The fact that Parnell moved out when the

children arrived is mentioned as an aside. Certainly the children were a great concern to Katharine.

This life in Brighton was a complete escape from political worries, and now from the problems, or indeed the blessings, presented by the impending divorce proceedings. Katharine says that they wondered whether:

> ... the time of waiting we had imposed upon ourselves [that Ireland might not risk the leadership which seemed her only hope] till the way could be opened to our complete union before the world, was not to be too long for our endurance.

In their stormy life, Brighton itself provided a shaky haven. One incident she recounted seemed symbolic of their lives at the time. A storm had arisen as they made their way down to the pier. Parnell helped her over the chain barriers to try out his newly designed float, which quickly shattered against the pier. He remarked that the whole pier would not last long. She clung to him to save herself from the storm winds. He picked her up and held her over the stormy sea saying, 'Oh, my wife, my wife, I believe I'll jump in with you, and we shall be free for ever', to which she replied, 'As you will, my only love, but the children?'

# 15

At the time of the divorce case, Parnell, at the age of forty-three, had been fifteen years in the House of Commons. St John Ervine described him thus:

> ... he had grown from a shy, stammering, nervous, and extraordinarily ignorant young man into one of the most powerful leaders in the history of English politics. The Irish party, which had been a disregarded and derided gang of amiable job-hunters when he joined it, was now an influential and highly-disciplined body of resolute and tireless patriots serving their country ... He had achieved unity where there had been disorder, and authority where there was none ... Self government for Ireland was no longer a matter for academic discussion on a Parliamentary off-day, but a practical proposal which might at any moment become a fact.

On 4 November 1890 Gladstone wrote to Arnold Morley:

> I fear a thundercloud is about to burst over Parnell's head, and I suppose it will end the career of a man in many respects invaluable.

Most of his party closed ranks behind him, feeling that the divorce case need not result in a loss of his leadership, a belief undoubtedly shared by Parnell himself. His one personal concern was to be free to marry Katharine at last, and he decided that neither of them should contest the case.

At the beginning of November 1890, both were served with copies of the petition in the case of O'Shea v. O'Shea — he at his solicitors' chambers and she at 10 Walsingham Terrace, Brighton.

The *Irish Times* of 17 November 1890 describes the opening of the case two days earlier:

> The great rush made to obtain seats at the hearing of this long awaited suit produced an eager throng at the entrance to Mr. Justice Butt's Court ... It had been circumstantially given out

> for months that Mr. Parnell had a complete answer to the
> charge ... would prove himself as immaculate and white as his
> own shirt front ... The janitors at the doors of the court were
> subjected to a perfect storm of importunistic reporters for
> whom seats had not apparently been provided. The statement,
> literally true, 'There isn't a seat for love nor money, gentlemen'
> was met with warm expostulation ... There were very few
> ladies present — only four all told — in the gallery, which was
> also crowded.

By coincidence, it was heard in the same court as the historical Special Commission, which must have given hope for a
repeat victory for Parnell, yet where was the man himself?
His solicitor, Mr George Lewis, was in court but left as soon
as proceedings started. When the judge asked 'Is anyone
appearing for Mr. Parnell?', no reply was given. Mr Frank
Lockwood said that he represented Mrs O'Shea but would
not be taking any part whatsoever in the proceedings —
would neither be calling witnesses nor cross-examining!

Captain O'Shea, 'neatly and quietly dressed and with
much of his old military smartness about him', sat in front of
his counsel with his son, Gerard, at his side, 'a fine bright-
complexioned young fellow, with fair hair, and an intellect-
ual head'.

The Solicitor General, Sir Edward Clarke, said that the
case stood undefended, but that he was bound to put suffic-
ient evidence before the jury, and that the pleadings were:

> ... so remarkable in their character that he should be doing
> injustice to Mr. O'Shea, whom he represented, if he did not
> occupy the court for some short time by stating matters which
> had become most material to his interests and his honour by
> reason of the defence put upon this record.

Both Parnell and Katharine had denied the charge, but then
she had made a counter charge of cruelty and neglect, and
suggested that he had connived at the adultery by encourag-
ing her to see Parnell. These charges had been withdrawn at
the last moment, but Katharine still said that Willie had

committed adultery with her own sister, Anna Steele, way back in 1881. His defence would be that there was 'not a word which can, in the slightest degree, support any of the charges'.

The *Irish Times* report continued with all the background to the marriage of Willie and Katharine, later corroborated by Willie's evidence: 'The parties seem to have lived a life of domestic happiness, except in regard to pecuniary matters', and had three children. In 1874, Katharine had gone to live at 'One Ash' [sic] Lodge to be near her Aunt, Mrs Wood, while Willie lived there when he was not away on business in Madrid 'and elsewhere'. It was not made clear either that this was due to their financial difficulties, or that it was her Aunt Ben who was supporting the family.

The story continued with Willie's election to Parliament and his introduction, at the Ennis Railway Station, to Parnell whom he invited to dine with himself, Katharine, Anna Steele and others. Until May 1881, when he heard rumours, he was entirely ignorant of Parnell's private visits to his wife. He immediately rushed to his home, found Parnell's portmanteau, which he took and threw out at Charing Cross Station, and challenged Parnell to a duel. His letter of challenge was read in court.

Anna Steele had intervened to stop the duel, and had gone to see Parnell at Westminster Hotel. 'He had assured her that there was no ground for Captain O'Shea's suspicions and Mrs. Steele saw Captain O'Shea and persuaded him to go to Eltham, where he interviewed Mrs. O'Shea, and there was a stormy and terrible scene'. Willie wrote to Parnell on 13 July 1881 (a date that was mentioned later in the case in relation to his supposed adultery with Anna Steele). After that, Willie went to Eltham with Anna and 'Mrs. O'Shea gave me assurances to such an extent that there was a reconciliation. I was convinced by Mrs. Steele that there was nothing wrong'. The result was that he and Katharine resumed their former relations.

Soon after this, Parnell had been imprisoned in Kilmainham, where Willie visited him and 'consulted in regard to political questions'. After his release his visits to Katharine resumed 'to an extent that attracted the attention of the elder children and the servants'.

Sir Edward Clarke continued to outline the case, telling how Parnell travelled to Eltham by different routes, breaking his journey as if to hide his destination. On visits to Wonersh Lodge, he slept in a bedroom joined to Katharine's by a dressing room. There and in other rooms they were heard talking together 'exceedingly late at night'. At times, Katharine had been away all night from the house, and on these occasions Parnell was not at Eltham. When the family went to Brighton, Captain O'Shea went also, but when he left there was a 'very constant and remarkable visitor', who was not mentioned often by name, and then referred to as Mr Smith, but was, without doubt, Parnell. Again here Katharine and he were regularly 'locked together in her bedroom', while Willie was entirely ignorant of these visits. In another house, Parnell was known as Mr Stuart, and 'he was always very careful to keep out of the way when Captain O'Shea came there'.

It must have been surprising to hear that Willie had copies of letters he had sent to Parnell. He had been away in Madrid and Portugal on business and heard that Parnell had been visiting his home again. Produced in court was a letter containing the following lines:

> You have behaved very badly to me. While I often told you that you were welcome to stay at Eltham whenever I was there I beg of you not to do so during my absence....

This was to prevent scandal. With renewed assurances from both parties, Willie's suspicions had been set aside.

Evidence would be given that a room was built on at the back of the house:

> ... apparently for Mr. Parnell's convenience of getting in ... It had a door to Mrs. O'Shea's boudoir. Mr. Parnell had a latch-

> key and used to let himself in through this new room and from
> time to time Mr. Parnell and Mrs. O'Shea were in that room,
> the door being locked. The son Gerard is in court and prepared
> to give evidence with regard to this matter ... in a most terrible
> position he behaved with great consideration for his mother,
> and at the same time, when he came to understand what was
> really going on, with loyalty to his father, and he showed him-
> self a lad of honour and of spirit....

Happily, the young lad was spared the traumatic experience of giving evidence.

Willie told of his election in Galway: of having been opposed by Healy and Biggar and of hearing further rumours about Katharine and Parnell: 'I remonstrated with my wife but she said that her acquaintance with Mr. Parnell was for political purposes'. Asked if Katharine told him anything about Parnell, he replied: 'Yes, she told me she knew he had been secretly married'.

When, in May 1886, the paragraph of innuendo had appeared in the *Pall Mall Gazette,* Willie had once more demanded to know what the article meant. He produced in court the letters from Katharine that ran: 'My Boysie, ... I have not the slightest idea what it means...', and from Parnell that stated: 'I am very sorry that you should have had any annoyance about the matter — I hope to see you on Sunday'. Later, when the *Sunday Daily News* hinted that Katharine and Parnell had been staying at Eastbourne, another letter from Katharine, also produced in court, was written: 'I know nothing about Mr. Parnell's movements in reference to Eastbourne and I do not see how I should be expected to ...', and another to her son: 'I am willing to meet your wishes with regard to Mr. Parnell. I agree that there shall be no further communication direct or indirect'.

It was heard in court how, in April 1887, the son, Gerard, came in the back way to the house and heard the voice of 'that awful scoundrel Parnell'. He asked his mother if it was he, and when she confirmed his suspicions by saying that Parnell had come to town, he thought it best to tell his father.

Through his solicitor Willie heard of 'Mrs. O'Shea's indign-ant denial that he had the least ground for his suspicion'.

In June of the same year, the report continues, Willie had read a paragraph in *The Times*, saying that Parnell was stay-ing in Brockley under the name of Preston. In the end of 1889, there were more items in newspapers about Katharine and Parnell.

The court heard how Katharine was living in a house in Brighton and, in December 1890, Willie:

> ... received information that led him to suspect that Parnell was living in the house and he therefore instructed his solicitor and the petition was filed on the 24th December.

Parnell and Katharine seemed indifferent to the reactions of the servants they employed. Perhaps they felt secure because they had lived under assumed names and in houses other than the family home. They little realised how soon their dis-guises had been unmasked, and that the servants had noted so many damning incidents.

First of these servants to give evidence was 'quietly dressed middle aged' Harriet Bull, 'of prim and severe aspect', who had worked for Katharine at 39 Bedford Square, Brighton. While she was in service, Parnell came every day to the house, 'at all times and stayed long when he came'. He and Katharine had been together in the drawing room and in her bedroom with the door locked. When he came the children were sent for drives.

Next into the box was the most talked about witness — '... [a] stout widow barely of middle age'. Caroline Pethers had worked as a cook for Katharine at 8 Medina Terrace, Hove (referred to as West Brighton), where Parnell had stayed under the name of Charles Stuart. He came and went from the house 'by the beach way' and he and Katharine went for drives — always at night time. The two would be locked in a room together for hours and, if the cook knocked, Katharine would open the door by an inch or two. On another occasion, Mrs Pethers and her husband watched from a higher landing as Mr Parnell retired to bed and Katharine followed him into his bedroom. The evidence continued:

> Captain O'Shea once called when Mr. Parnell was in the drawing room. It was dark and Mrs. O'Shea would not have the gas lighted, and witness went down stairs. Immediately afterwards Captain O' Shea rang the street door bell and came in, and a few minutes later Mr. Parnell, who had not come down the stairs knocked at the front door and asked to see Captain O'Shea. There were two rope fire escape ladders in the house (Laughter).

In his book on Parnell, St. John Irvine relates that, one night after the divorce case, Sir Hubert Tree was entertaining Willie, whose account of the story concluded: 'and the fun of it is there was no fire escape.' St. John Irvine continues: '… it appeared that the servant, explaining Parnell's swift disappearance, had used the words "fire escape" as one might use the expression "flown away on wings"'. This peculiar explanation casts grave doubt on that particular piece of evidence which was repeated over and over and was used to deride Parnell and Katharine on many an occasion.

Mrs Pethers was the last witness to appear that day, and the case was adjourned. After the first day's hearing Gladstone wrote to Morley:

> It is, after all, a thunderclap about Parnell. Will he ask for the Chiltern Hundreds? He cannot continue to lead....

# 16

The proceedings continued on Monday, 17 November, and reports continued in the *Irish Times* of the following day: 'There was naturally a warm demand for sittings within the court, all of which had, as matter of fact, been allotted days before'. The ushers' pleas for restraint met with demands to be squeezed in:

> It was of no use protesting or to dart angry looks at the intruders for the persistency with which they insinuated them-selves on the edges of the benches, in the gangways and else-where, was not only more than sufficient to provoke irritation, but to induce the use of language far stronger than parlia-mentary!

Willie and Gerard were there, of course, and Anna Steele with other members of Katharine's family — her brother, General Sir Evelyn Wood V.C. and her sister, Lady Barrett-Lennard. The thick November fog had 'penetrated the court, but the brilliancy of the electric light dissipated, to a great extent, the murky gloom and discovered the ladies to be very quietly attired in black'.

The Judge came into court at 11 o'clock and announced that it was not practice to accept photographs as a means of identification. The Solicitor General replied that he had sub-poenaed Mr Parnell, which caused a stir, but he assured the judge that he thought that his identity would be in no doubt when the evidence was heard.

The first witness that day was Jane Glenister, 'a young, self-possessed and somewhat voluble woman', who gave evidence of Parnell's visits to Eltham and Brighton from 1880 to 1882. She was followed by a waitress, Jane Chapman, who said that Parnell had been with Katharine all the time for the months of July and August of 1885, 'at times in a room with the door locked and … they often stayed out late'.

The accident that led to the article in the *Pall Mall Gazette* was described by the coachman, Richard Wise, and this story was corroborated by his relative, Thomas Partridge, who had since enlisted, and appeared in court in cavalry uniform.

Those acting for Willie had gone to great lengths to find these servants, who were followed by a number of house agents — Mr Samuel Locke of Eastbourne, who was not concerned who lived in the houses he let; Mr Ernest Vinall, also of Eastbourne, who was more curious and had sent his agreement to Westminster; Mr George Porter, who let the house at Brockley and who related the tale of Parnell forgetting which name he had used; Mr Yates, who let the house in Regent's Park, and caused amusement when he said that Katharine had used Parnell's name as a reference (in this instance Parnell had gone under the name of O'Shea). Other names Parnell used were listed. A sad story emerged, each shred of evidence seeming more damning than the last.

Saddest of all witnesses called was Anna Steele:

> 'You are the sister of Mrs. O'Shea, the respondent?'
> 'Yes.'
> 'In the respondent's particulars it is alleged that Captain O'Shea committed adultery with you on or about the 13th or 14th July 1881. Is there one word of truth in that charge?'
> 'Not one.'
> 'Then, nor at any time?'
> 'Not at any time.'
> 'That is all I ask you.'

This concluded the evidence, but one of the jurors asked for further clarification of the counter charges, now withdrawn, of cruelty and neglect. Willie was recalled to the witness box.

The Solicitor General stated that Willie had lived at Albert Mansions while his wife lived at Wonersh Lodge and asked, was this:

> '... at your wife's desire and at your aunt's wish?'
> 'Certainly.'
> 'Were you, during the whole of that time on affectionate terms with your wife?'

'Perfectly.'

'You produce a number of letters and your wife produces 700!'

'Yes, we were in constant communication.'

'Did you used to go down to Eltham?'

'Constantly, and she came up to town and dined with me.'

'Now in any of the letters did she ever complain of the arrangements which had been made?'

'Never.'

'Is there any pretence for saying that you ever neglected your wife or treated her with unkindness?'

'Never. I was never away from my wife for one week without her consent and approval.'

The brave juror was not to be quietened:

'Were you wholly responsible for the maintenance of your family, and did you look after the children and see that they were properly educated?'

'Certainly, and I was at home constantly.'

The juror had got 'firmly fixed in his modicum of mind the good old British doctrine of domesticity, that it is the first duty of a husband to sleep nightly in the bosom of his family':

'What do you mean, sir, by constantly? Did you return home every night?'

'Certainly not. I was in Parliament, and when there I naturally would not go home every night. No one had made the slightest complaint about any inattention on my part. The Solicitor-General has every proof in my diaries of my having been a most kind husband and father.'

The 'amateur lawyer, who had strayed into the dozen of good men and true', continued to cross-examine Willie:

'How do you account for your conduct in having challenged Mr. Parnell to a duel, and then again inviting him for dinner?'

'Because it was made perfectly clear to me at the time that there was no foundation for any suspicions.'

'I believe letters passed between you and your wife as to

105

money matters. Why were they not produced?'
'They are in court.'

The juror pressed once more:

'Is it a fact that the journey to Wonersh Lodge is done in an hour?'
'Yes, and I constantly did it.'

The judge summed up:

'... it is an immoral, improper and reprehensible thing to indulge in an intimacy of this sort with a married woman whether the husband was a consenting party or not....' As to the charge of adultery brought by Mrs. O'Shea, it was simply shocking. There did not appear to be a shadow of foundation for it, and she had discredited her own sister. That was a matter he need not trouble the jury with. He simply asked them, first, had the adultery charged between the respondent and the co-respondent been committed: and secondly, had there been any connivance of that adultery on the part of the petitioner?

After one minute the jury reached a verdict: both counts went against Katharine and Parnell, with costs. Custody of the two youngest children was awarded to Willie.

Two telegrams were printed in the *Irish Times* immediately after the report of the case. The first:

London, Monday.

We understand that the belief generally prevails among the members of the Irish party at present in this country or in Ireland that recent events will not necessitate any change in the leadership of the Home Rule movement. The enormous services which Mr. Parnell has rendered to the Irish cause should, it is thought, be allowed to atone for any irregularities in the honourable gentleman's private life. If there is to be any change or proposed change in the leadership of the Parliamentary party the initiative will come from Mr. Parnell himself.

The second:

> New York, Monday.
>
> Mr. Eugene Keely, a prominent New York Irishman, and treas-
> urer of the fund which is being raised by the Irish delegates,
> has declared that should Mr. Parnell be proved guilty of the
> charges brought against him by Captain O'Shea neither the
> clergy nor the laity of America would have any more to do
> with him.

The *Daily Telegraph* of 17 November said:

> ... the effect of this trial will be to relegate Mr. Parnell for a
> time, at any rate, to private life ... Special exemptions from
> penalties which should apply to all public men alike cannot
> possibly be made in favour of exceptionally valuable politi-
> cians to suit the convenience of their parties. He must cease, for
> the present, at any rate, to lead the nationalist party ... It is no
> satisfaction to us to feel that a political adversary whose abil-
> ities and prowess it was impossible not to respect, has been
> overthrown by irrelevant accident, wholly unconnected with
> the struggle in which we are engaged.

Parnell undoubtedly felt that the divorce case was politically
irrelevant. The very day Katharine's solicitor brought her a
copy of the decree nisi, the Irish papers carried a letter from
him urging Irish members to attend the opening of the new
session at Westminster, as '... the coming session will be one
of combat from first to last'.

The Irish Catholic clergy were slow to comment: Parnell
was not of their faith, and they expected that he would
resign, even for a while. On 17 November, Archbishop
Croke wrote to Davitt: 'A leader is one who leads — and
Parnell has not led for the last half a dozen years'.

Gladstone wrote, on 18 November, to Morley:

> I had noticed the Parnell circular, not without misgiving. I read
> ... a noteworthy article in the *Daily Telegraph* with which I very
> much agree. But I think it plain that we have nothing to say
> and nothing to do in this matter ... I own to some surprise at

the apparent facility with which the R.C. bishops and clergy appear to take the continued leadership, but they may have tried the ground and found it would not bear. It is the Irish parliamentary party, and that alone to which we have to look....

The editorial in the *Freeman's Journal* of 18 November boldly declared: 'He is Leader and he shall remain Leader.'

# 17

The fortnightly meeting of the National League was held on 18 November, the day after the verdict. Most of those who attended were on Parnell's side. The meeting was chaired by John Redmond, who declared:

> The Irish Party are bound to their leader by ties of absolute confidence and unquestioning loyalty. If he was thinking of quitting, the Irish people would come as one man and entreat him not to desert them....

Others who might have opposed him were in America on a fund raising mission, with the exception of Healy, who, when he had spoken out against Parnell in Galway, had been ignored. Moreover, when a further meeting was held in the Leinster Hall on 20 November, a very ill Healy made an impassioned plea for his leader:

> For Ireland and for Irishmen, Mr. Parnell is less a man than an institution. We have, under the shadow of his name, secured a power and authority in the councils of Great Britain and the world such as we never possessed before ... I say we would be foolish and criminal if we surrendered the great chief who had led us so far forward ... if we join with this howling pack, would that be a noble spectacle before the nations?

McCarthy, who chaired that meeting, read a telegram from the American party, which included Dillon and O'Brien:

> We stand firmly by the leadership of the man who has brought the Irish people through unparalleled difficulties and dangers, from servitude and despair to the very threshold of emancipation, with a genius, courage and success unequalled in our story. We do so, not only on the ground of gratitude for these imperishable services in the past, but in the profound conviction that Parnell's statesmanship and matchless qualities as a leader are essential to the safety of our cause.

The Irish party seemed to be solidly behind him.

The Irish bishops were taken aback by the support at this meeting. Archbishop Croke, who had been an ardent supporter, threw out a bust of Parnell he had had in his hall. He felt that the Irish party disregarded the clergy and treated them only as money gatherers. On 4 December 1890, the Bishops issued a manifesto in which they stated:

> ... without hesitation, or doubt and in the plainest terms, we give it as our unanimous judgement that whoever else is fit to fill that highly responsible post [head of the Irish Parliamentary Party] Mr. Parnell decidedly is not....

Of all the Irish party, Michael Davitt was the first to foresee that the English party would demand Parnell's resignation. In an article in the *Labour World* of 20 November, he wrote:

> The question for Mr. Parnell is — is he going to put the loyalty of the Irish people to a test which will disintegrate the forces behind the home rule cause in Britain?

The English Liberal Party, which had its annual general meeting on 20–21 November, made their views known to Gladstone. According to Morley, letters poured in to him: 'Temporal withdrawal, said some; permanent withdrawal, said others, but all for withdrawal of some sort, almost all were inexorable'. A written report from the Liberal Party meeting ran:

> ... the opinion was absolutely unanimous and extremely strong that, if Parnell is allowed to remain as the leader of the Irish party, all further co-operation between them and the English liberals must be at an end....

Gladstone waited to see if Parnell would contact him, and wrote to Morley on 24 November:

> I thought it necessary ... to acquaint Mr. McCarthy with the conclusion ... that notwithstanding the splendid services rend-

ered by Mr. Parnell to his country, his continuance at the present moment in the leadership would be productive of consequences disastrous in the highest degree to the cause of Ireland ... This explanation of my views I begged Mr. McCarthy to regard as confidential, and not intended for his colleagues generally, if he found that Mr. Parnell contemplated spontaneous action; but I also begged that he would make known to the Irish party, at their meeting to-morrow afternoon, that such was my conclusion, if he should find that Mr. Parnell had not in contemplation any step of the nature indicated....

In case McCarthy did not get to Parnell, Gladstone urged Morley to see him before the election took place for leader of the Irish Party, and to make these views known to him.

As it turned out, Parnell did not put in an appearance until the last moment before the meeting in Committee Room 15. Morley could not speak to him, but McCarthy gave him Gladstone's message. Parnell said that he would, 'stand to his guns'. In spite of Gladstone's instructions, no other member of the Irish party was told, and Parnell entered the meeting, looking, as his followers said, 'as if we had committed adultery with his wife'! He was re-elected as leader and, when he met Morley shortly afterwards, told him that it was a 'storm in a tea-cup', and would soon pass. Morley insisted that it would be the ruin of Home Rule. Parnell replied that, if he left the leadership, he would not return, and added: 'Of course Mr. Gladstone will have to attack me. I shall expect that. He will have a right to do that'.

Morley reported this to Gladstone who immediately decided to send a copy of his letter to the press. The reporters had it by 8 p.m. and word spread quickly through the House of Commons. The Irish Party did not know how to take it — they had worked for five years with the British. As Morley describes it:

They suddenly learned that if they took a certain step in respect of the leadership of their own party, the alliance was broken off, the most powerful of Englishmen could help them no more....

Parnell sat alone in the smoking room of the House of Commons.

On the following day, 26 November 1890, the Irish party held another meeting. John Barry immediately proposed that Parnell, who was in the chair, should retire from leadership. Many agreed. The meeting was adjourned until 1 December, and Parnell hurried home to Katharine:

> … he came over to me, and took me into his arms, saying 'I think we shall have to fight, Queenie. Can you bear it? I'm afraid it is going to be tough work.' I said 'Yes, if you can.' But I must confess that when I looked at the frail and white face that was so painfully delicate, whose only vitality seemed to lie in the deep, burning eyes, my heart misgave me, for I very much doubted if his health would stand any prolonged strain.
>
> I loved him so much, and I did so long to take him away from all the ingratitude and trouble — to some sunny land where we could forget the world and be forgotten. But then I knew that he would not forget; that he would come at my bidding, but that his desertion of Ireland would lie at his heart; that if he was to be happy he must fight to the end. I knew him too well to dare to take him away from the cause he had made his life-work; that even if it killed him I must let him fight — fight to the end — it was himself — the great self that I loved, and that I would not spoil even through my love, though it might bring the end in death.

It being winter, Parnell suffered from rheumatism and had an almost continuous pain in his left arm. 'I am feeling very ill, Queenie, but I think I shall win through', he said, 'I shall never give in unless you make me, and I want you to promise me that you will never make me less than the man you have known'.

# 18

On the night of Friday, 28 November 1890, at the home in Chester Place of Dr FitzGerald, Parnell called a meeting of a few of his supporters, and read the manifesto he had written in reply to Gladstone. He began:

> To the People of Ireland.
>
> The integrity and independence of a section of the Irish Parliamentary party has been sapped and destroyed by the wire-pullers of the English Liberal party....

Horgan, who was a loyal supporter of Parnell, describes it as:

> ... a fierce and indeed unfair, manifesto in which he disclosed the purport of his confidential talks with Gladstone and Morley and charged the Liberal leaders with an attempt to cheat the Irish people out of a full measure of Home Rule — although he had in fact, shortly after these interviews, publicly expressed his confidence in Gladstone. This, he told the Irish, was the measure of the loss with which they were threatened unless they consented to throw him to the English wolves now howling for his destruction. These were terrible and decisive words which made any compromise impossible.

It was published in the papers of the following morning. Later in the day, Archbishop Croke telegraphed Justin McCarthy, to say that Parnell should retire 'quietly and with good grace'. Not so quietly, Archbishop Walsh made his views known in the *Freeman's Journal* of 1 December:

> If the Irish leader would not or could not, give a public assurance that his honour was unsullied, the party that takes him or retains him as its leader can no longer count on the support of the bishops of Ireland.

On that fateful first day of December, the Irish party gathered in Committee Room 15 to begin days of debate on the whole question. Reports of this meeting appeared in many newspapers, including the *Freeman's Journal* (5 December), *United Ireland* (13 December), and the *Belfast Evening Telegraph* (8 December).

In Tim Healy's mind, rankled Parnell's rejection of his services in the forgery case, and his became one of the stronger voices against Parnell.

Parnell deftly managed to turn the talk from his divorce case to the points he had made in his manifesto. Many and varied speeches were made, and on 3 December, J.J. Clancy, in the absence of Parnell, made the following proposal:

> That in view of the difference of opinion that has arisen between Mr. Gladstone and Mr. Parnell as to the accuracy of Mr. Parnell's recollection of the suggestions offered at Hawarden in reference to suggested changes in, and departures from the Home Rule Bill of 1886 on the subject of the control of the constabulary and the settlement of the land question, the Whips of the party be instructed to obtain from Mr. Gladstone, Mr. John Morley and Sir William Harcourt for the information of the party, before any further consideration of the question, what their views are with regard to these two vital points.

Parnell, on his return, said that he had no time to think over this proposal, and asked for an adjournment until the following day. At this point, Tim Healy rose to his feet and said:

> I wish to make a personal declaration in your regard, Mr. Parnell. I wish to say that if you feel able to meet the party on these points, my voice will be the first, on the very earliest moment possible, consonant with the liberties of my country, to call you back to your proper place as the leader of the Irish race.

He wept. Parnell said not a word.

On the following day, he was soon on his feet, making a speech in answer to the suggestions. With regard to Gladstone, he said:

> ... if I surrender to him, if I give up my position to him, if you throw me to him, I say gentlemen, that it is your bounden duty to see that you secure value for the sacrifice! ... and upon that answer I will stand or fall before the country.

'Then you will fall, Mr. Parnell ...' said Healy.

The exchanges became angry and wounding. Healy quoted an earlier speech by Parnell, relating to the alliance between the Liberals and the Irish party, in which he had referred to it as, 'an alliance which I venture to believe will last'. Healy asked, 'What broke it off?' and received a general reply: 'Gladstone's letter'. Bitterly, Healy corrected them: 'It perished in the stench of the divorce court'.

The stops had now all been pulled out — or had they? What worse could be said? A delegation had been sent to Gladstone to hear his views on a future Home Rule Bill. Gladstone told them that his views on Home Rule were well known and that he would discuss nothing further with them until they had decided on a leader. This news, brought back to the meeting on 6 December, elicited from John Redmond a statement that Parnell was 'the master of the party', to which Healy retorted: 'Who is to be the mistress of the party?'

For once, Parnell's composure was shaken. He rose to his feet. A member cried, 'I appeal to my friend the chairman ...', but Parnell interrupted in rage: 'Better appeal to your own friend, better appeal to that cowardly little scoundrel there, that in an assembly of Irishmen dares to insult a woman.'

All hope of unity had vanished. Shortly after this exchange, Justin McCarthy rose to say that he could see no point in continuing further, and asked all those who agreed with him to withdraw from the meeting. He and 44 other members left the room, leaving only 26 Parnell supporters. Defiantly, Parnell spoke of the seceders:

> ... the position of men who, having taken pledges to be true to their party, to be true to their leaders, to be true to their coun-

try, have been false to all these pledges.

The men to whom he was referring went to the conference room of the House of Commons and unanimously passed a resolution that:

> ... acting under an imperative sense of duty to our country, we, the undersigned, being an absolute majority of the whole number of the Irish Parliamentary party, declare that Mr. Parnell's term of chairmanship of this party is hereby terminated.

The Irish party was completely divided.

Justin McCarthy was nominated leader of the group which met later that day to launch a new paper to replace the *Freeman's Journal*, which they considered to be very biased in Parnell's favour. Tim Healy devoted much of his time in the ensuing months to this project. The anti-Parnellites called themselves the National Committee.

# 19

Katharine wrote that Parnell's 'outlook was so much wider than is generally understood and his comment on members of the Party was always, both before and after the split, calm, considerate, and as being impersonal to himself'. He did not feel resentful to Gladstone and said to her, 'You don't make allowances for statecraft'. His attitude to the Irish Catholic clergy was:

> They have to obey their bishops, and they have to obey Rome — and that's why the whole system of their interference is so infernal....

Certainly, Parnell did not consider the fight was over. On 9 December, he returned to Dublin at the same time as Tim Healy. Great crowds gathered to cheer Parnell. When Healy was recognised someone shouted, 'A groan for the Chief Justice', who left amid jeers of contempt. Despite the early hour, brass bands greeted Parnell, and he received an address of welcome. At Brunswick Street, the horse was taken from his carriage and he was drawn by the excited crowd to the home of Dr Kenny in Rutland Square. Katharine Tynan wrote:

> The leader was simply drinking in thirstily this immense love, which must have been more heartening than one can say after that bitter time in the English capital.

That night, he went to the Rotunda and was joined along the way by the Lord Mayor of Dublin. The following is St. John Ervine's account:

> Bands and torch-bearers were in front of the procession ... In the Rotunda itself an immovable mass of cheering men and women were packed. The enthusiasm in the street flowed into the hall, and threw the audience into a ferment of devotion ... He was no longer the smartly-dressed man as he had formerly

been. He stooped slightly and his untrimmed hair was turning grey and scanty. His pale face was paler than usual, but his eyes retained their fire. He spoke for an hour ... and moved his people as he pleased.

The voice of Parnell rang out:

I don't intend to plead to you here to-night excuses or reasons for my action, believing that you have confidence in me, and will not put me through the ordeal of excuses or reasons, but that you will take me for what you know me to be, for what you believe me to be, and for what, please God, I will prove myself to be in the face of Ireland and of my fellow-countrymen ... I don't pretend that I had not moments of trial and of temptation, but I do claim that never in thought, word, or deed have I been false to the trust Irishmen have confided in me.

While this speech was being given, the anti-Parnellites chose to raid the premises of the United Irishmen. Word came to Parnell the next morning at breakfast, and he decided to regain possession. He ran from his carriage, hammered on the door, and when no reply was forthcoming, a pickaxe and crowbar were produced by his followers. A passer-by told of what followed:

Now Parnell snatched the crowbar, and, swinging his arms with might and main, thundered at the door. The door yielded ... What happened within the house I do not know ... One of the windows on the second storey was removed, and Parnell suddenly appeared in the aperture. He had conquered. The enthusiasm which greeted him cannot be described ... The closing words of his speech still ring in my ear: 'I rely on Dublin. Dublin is true. What Dublin says to-day Ireland will say to-morrow.'

According to Katharine, Parnell said: 'It was splendid fun. I wish I could burgle my own premises every day!'

At this time, a parliamentary vacancy occurred in North Kilkenny. Parnell decided to fight Sir John Pope Hennessy, the anti-Parnellite candidate. He went to Cork to ask his old friend, M.J. Horgan, to run the campaign. Arriving there on

11 December, he was given his usual warm welcome. Horgan's son takes up the story:

> He stayed at my father's house that night and I shall never forget his appearance as I saw him standing before the fire in the dining-room just after he arrived. He looked like a hunted fugitive, his hair dishevelled, his beard unkempt, his eyes wild and restless. My father made some vehement remark about those who had deserted him, and the hatred in Parnell's face was terrible to look upon.

No longer was he 'calm' and 'considerate' to these people, as Katharine suggests.

Parnell had asked R. Barry O'Brien to stand in North Kilkenny, but O'Brien had said that he would prefer not, as he did not have the money. Parnell offered, if necessary, to provide this. At the last moment Vincent Scully, a wealthy and influential Tipperary Catholic landlord, agreed to contest the election. O'Brien was not notified, and travelled to Kilkenny. When he arrived, Parnell and his party had taken over the Victoria Hotel (replaced in 1921-2 by the present day Allied Irish Bank, High Street). Everyone spoke in whispers, as the Chief was asleep on some chairs before the fire. O'Brien thought he looked like a dying man, and was told that he was ill, but that it was hoped that a night's rest would 'set him up'.

The campaign took days, during which they all worked tirelessly in very bad weather conditions, and with little sleep. According to Healy, Parnell 'passed from one end of the constituency to the other like a whirlwind, smiting his opponents as he passed'. He called Davitt a jackdaw, Dillon a peacock, Healy himself a scoundrel and a traitor, while others were the scum of creation.

In Castlecomer, lime was thrown in Parnell's eyes. However, not everyone was as violent, and a local supporter, Dr J. Byrne Hackett, licked the lime from Parnell's eyes, believing that saliva would be the best remedy. 'The newspapers made the most of the affair and I thought my husband was blinded', writes Katharine. Parnell asked a supporter to send a telegram on his behalf to reassure her, but the message was torn from the man's hand, and she was distracted until she finally got his reassurance that he was not injured.

In their speeches, Healy and company derided 'Kitty' O'Shea at every opportunity. After the Kilkenny election, Parnell said that 'it would have really hurt if those devils had got hold of your real name, My Queenie, or even the 'Katie' or 'Dick' that your relations and Willie called you', because, as she added, 'my name was Katharine'.

The American delegates sent messages of support for Hennessy, not so much to defeat Parnell as to encourage his temporary resignation, but it was the clergy who did the most to influence the people. On 22 December 1890, Hennessy received 2,527 votes — over 1,000 votes more than Scully's 1,362. It was a bitter defeat, but Parnell promised to continue the fight, even travelling to Dublin that night for a meeting outside the National Club.

The American delegation hoped for a reconciliation, but they were unaware of the full facts. William O'Brien arrived in Boulogne with proposals from the American group that Parnell should retire for a period only. O'Brien was a wanted man and would be arrested if he came to Ireland, so Parnell went to meet him in France.

Pro- and anti-Panellites had their say, but Parnell would not accept the terms of the agreement. The old arguments were raised about Gladstone, the leadership of the parliamentary party, the chairmanship of the National League. Parnell, still seeking assurances from the Liberals, wanted only O'Brien and himself to be judges of the assurances — McCarthy was to have no voice.

Dillon returned from America at the end of January. Parnell refused him access to Irish party funds in France.

Gladstone wrote to Lord Acton that he was:

> ... chained to the spot by this Parnell business, and every day have to consider in one shape or other what ought to be said by

> myself or others ... I consider the Parnell chapter of politics finally closed for us, the British liberals, at least during my time. He has been even worse since the divorce court than he was in it. The most astounding revelation of my lifetime.

Within a few months, Parnell put up a candidate in Sligo, who was defeated. A third constituency, Carlow, had a vacancy caused by the death of The O'Gorman Mahon who, ironically, had been involved in bringing Katharine and Parnell together. His candidate for Carlow was an old Land Leaguer, and even he was reluctant to stand.

Parnell wore himself out in all these campaigns, travelling up and down the country, crossing to England weekly to see Katharine, and making journeys to France. Meanwhile, the tide of opinion was turning against him.

According to Katharine:

> ... as regards the marriage bond his honest conviction was that there is none where intense mutual attraction — commonly called love — does not exist, or where it ceases to exist. To Parnell's heart and conscience I was no more the wife of Captain O'Shea when he first met me than I was after Captain O'Shea had divorced me, ten years later.

Parnell could not see why he was condemned. Had Katharine divorced O'Shea before or when she met Parnell, public opinion would not have gone so strongly against him. While it is possible that a man married to a divorcee might not have been acceptable as leader of the Irish party, it was the years of apparent deception that appalled his followers — three of his children baptised and reared as O'Sheas — and the constant changes of name and address indeed seemed sordid.

W.B. Yeats was sure of the cause of Parnell's downfall:

> The Bishops and the Party
> That tragic story made,
> A husband that had sold his wife
> And after that betrayed;

But stories that live longest
Are sung above the glass,
And Parnell loved his country,
And Parnell loved his lass.

# 20

The couple had to wait until June 1891 to be legally free to marry. The day before the wedding, Parnell made his will, on a double sheet of foolscap in his own handwriting. He bequeathed Avondale and all he possessed to Katharine and their two daughters. Unfortunately, his knowledge of law was scant — he should have re-executed it later, as the marriage invalidated the will.

On 25 June, he tapped on Katharine's door at day-break, calling: 'Get up, get up, it is time to be married!' He had given out instructions to a servant to take Dictator out with the carriage at eleven so that this would be leaked to reporters who would be thrown off the scent. Long before this hour, the household was agog with excitement — two loyal and trusted servants who were to have the privilege of acting as witnesses were packed off to await the couple at the Steyning registrar's office. Parnell and Katharine exchanged white roses. One of the servants had already pinned a posy of flowers to her dress, but this was replaced by Parnell's with the promise that the others would be carried as a bouquet.

Parnell took little interest in clothes, but that morning as he climbed into the carriage he exclaimed: 'Queenie, you look lovely in that lace stuff and the beautiful hat with the roses! I am so proud of you!' The driver, who had expected an eleven o'clock ceremony, was barely awake for the six o'clock nine-mile journey.

Dictator travelled so quickly that they arrived ahead of the train, and Parnell admired them both in the little mirror of the registrar's office, saying: 'It isn't every woman who makes so good a marriage as you are making, Queenie, is it? and to such a handsome fellow, too!' Flowers decorated the little room and,  once the witnesses had arrived, the little ceremony, that was to legalise the union of so many years, was soon over.

Safe in the carriage again, Parnell pulled up the hood saying: 'It's the right thing to do. How could I kiss you good wishes for our married life unless we were hooded up like this!' as they galloped past the newspaper men.

More press men had gathered at Walsingham Terrace, and Parnell said, with some satisfaction: 'Stand back; let Mrs. Parnell pass! Presently, presently; I'll see you presently!' and when one of the servants asked if Mrs O'Shea would see a reporter, Parnell exclaimed in a horrified voice: 'What do you mean? WHO is Mrs. O'Shea?'

After a 'dainty little wedding breakfast', without wedding cake as he did not like it, Parnell sat in his easy chair, watching his bride who asked why he watched her so. He replied, savouring the title 'wife': 'Why not? A cat may look at a king, and surely a man may look at his wife!' As it was a lovely June day, they wandered across the fields to Aldrington, and sat looking out to sea, making plans for when Ireland would have:

> ... settled down, and my King ... in forcing reason upon that unreasonable land and wresting the justice of Home Rule from England — could abdicate; when we could go to find a better climate, so that his health might become all I wished. We talked of the summer visits we would make to Avondale, and of the glorious days when he need never go away from me ... we sat together, silent now, even though we spoke together still with the happiness that has no words ... Reading my thoughts, he said '... there is nothing in the wide world that can be greater than our love; there is nothing in all the world but you and I.'

The Parnell family welcomed Katharine into its ranks, especially his mother.

At the time of his wedding, the *Freeman's Journal*, which had so long supported him, withdrew its support.

The Carlow election took place soon after the wedding, and in the months that followed whenever Parnell was campaigning, he telegraphed Katharine morning and night, and wrote her letters when he could snatch time — a scarce commodity. Failure in Carlow did not deter his efforts as he drove himself relentlessly.

Many could not understand his frantic behaviour. In an article on Parnell in the *Irish Medical Times* of 25 January 1991, Dr Sean Callan suggests that the Parnell family suffered from Bi-polar Affective illness (Thomas Parnell, way back in the eighteenth century, showed signs of manic depression, and Henry Parnell, the following century, hanged himself). In Callan's opinion:

> Inheriting the gene in DNA may account for Parnell's prodigious energy, high work tolerance and optimism on one hand and his recurrent episodes of sleep disturbance, anorexia, 'torpid' liver and variable temperament on the other. Affective illness clouds judgements which may have sown the seeds for Parnell's eventual political demise ... In short, his bi-polar DNA was both his boon and his bane.

During these months, Parnell became friendly again with Justin McCarthy, but they did not discuss the split. Some areas received him better than others. In Limerick, one of his successes, he insisted on giving his speech, standing on the window sill of Cruise's Hotel, with his followers holding him by his coat tails, and in Cabinteely, he spoke bareheaded, in the pouring rain.

His last meeting with R. Barry O'Brien was at Euston Station. He asked O'Brien what he thought would be the result of the next general election. 'I should think that you will come back with about five followers', was the reply, 'and I should not be surprised if you came back absolutely alone.' 'Well,' remarked Parnell, 'if I do come back absolutely alone, one thing is certain, I shall then represent a party whose independence will not be sapped'.

In spite of the brave face, Parnell wrote to his mother:

> I am weary, dear mother, of these troubles, weary unto death; but it is all in a good cause. With health and the assistance of my friends I am confident of the result....

On 27 September 1891, at Creggs, on the Roscommon-Galway border, Parnell attended his last public meeting, He was very ill, his arm in a sling, and his doctor urged him not to go. He had, however, given his word and, as always, kept it. In driving rain, someone opened an umbrella over him, but he insisted it be put down. Utterly exhausted, he arrived at the home of his friend, Dr Kenny, where he spent three days discussing the establishment of a new newspaper, *The Irish Daily Independent*.

Although in great pain, he insisted on going home, stopping only to have a Turkish bath in London. After his last speech he had remained in his damp clothes and footwear, as his famous little bag had been taken in error by one of his hosts. Katharine was very worried when she saw how ill he looked, and he greeted her: 'Oh, my Wifie, it is good to be back. You may keep me a bit now!'

That night he sat by the fire, stroking Katharine's hair, but had to be helped up the stairs. In the course of the next few days he weakened considerably. In one of his occasional good periods, Katharine showed him an engraving of a picture called 'Wedded', which amused him. She urged him to call Sir Henry Thompson, but he wrote instead, while a local doctor ministered to him.

Late on Tuesday 6 October 1891, Parnell opened his eyes and said, 'Kiss me, sweet Wifie, and I will try to sleep a little'. Katharine continues:

> I lay down by his side, and kissed the burning lips he pressed to mine for the last time. The fire of them, fierce beyond any I had ever felt, even in his most loving moods, startled me, and as I slipped my hand from under his head he gave a little sigh and became unconscious. The doctor came at once, but no remedies prevailed against this sudden failure of the heart's action, and my husband died without regaining consciousness, before his last kiss was cold on my lips ... His face was so peaceful; so well, all the tiredness had gone from it now ... And the rain and the wind swept about the house as though the whole world shared my desolation.

The cause of death was given as rheumatic fever, with a rider that the heart was weak — there was no post mortem. Later suggestions include a sudden infection, lobar pneumonia, kidney failure (Bright's disease), or cancer, while the painful left arm would have been rheumatic. No death mask was made as the body temperature was too high, and his body had to be placed in a lead casket. The rose that he had kept since stooping to retrieve it at their very first meeting, Katharine now placed on her beloved's breast before the coffin was closed.

Katharine was reluctant to agree to a public funeral, but five days after his death, Ireland's dead chief was met by an enormous crowd in Dublin. The body lay in state in the City Hall, before being escorted to Glasnevin cemetery. W.F. Denning wrote to *The Observatory* about a bright falling star seen at the time of the burial:

> [a] very fine meteor was observed at several stations on Sunday Oct. 11, 6.30 (p.m.) ... Mr. E.M. Richards of Enniscorthy, Ireland, describes the meteor as much larger and brighter than Jupiter and of a bluish-white colour ... It disappeared in a shower of sparks ... after a duration of 4 seconds. Other correspondents describe the meteor as remarkably brilliant, lighting up the sky like a flash of lightning.

Maud Gonne wrote in her autobiography: '... as the thud of the earth sounded on the coffin, a rift in the leaden sky parted the clouds and a bright falling star was seen'. She told W.B. Yeats (he hated crowds and did not attend the funeral), and he later wrote in 'Parnell's Funeral':

> A bundle of tempestuous cloud is blown
> About the sky; where that is clear of cloud
> brightness remains; a brighter star shoots down....

Despite the enormous funeral, Parnell's grave remained neglected for a very long time and Katharine, was distracted by this. She was long dead when, nearly fifty years after his death, the few of his remaining party and their descendants erected a great unhewn stone of Wicklow granite, inscribed with the one word, 'Parnell'.

# 21

Katharine was ill from grief after Parnell's death. That grief was exacerbated just three weeks later when Tim Healy, in a public speech in Longford, once more referred to her as a 'proved British prostitute'. The gallantry of the Parnell family had not died with Parnell. His nephew, Alfred Tudor MacDermott — the son of his sister, Sophia — then a twenty-three-year-old engineering student at Trinity, was incensed. On 4 November 1891, the day after Healy's speech was reported in the newspapers, Alfred waylaid and horse-whipped him from the Four Courts library to the coffee room.

An article in the *Irish Times* of 5 November 1891, refers to the incident in a report on a meeting held in the Nationalist Club 'for the purpose of arranging for the presentation of an address to Mr. Tudor MacDermott in recognition of his manly conduct in publicly horse-whipping Mr. Timothy Healy'. Telegrams of support were read from Cork, Waterford and Belfast, and a sub-committee was appointed to 'select a suitable whip to be mounted in gold and inscribed'.

At that time, Norah O'Shea, Willie's second child, and Clare and Katie, daughters of Parnell, lived with Katharine. Willie had been given legal custody of Parnell's children, as it was assumed by the court that they were his, but he had not claimed this right.

Six months later, Aunt Ben's will was due to be contested. Two days before the case, Anna Steele visited Katharine and brought with her a letter from Willie:

Dear Katie,

I think that you are worrying yourself unnecessarily about the custody of Clare and Katie because, having regard to the reasonable attitude of your Counsel on the application before the Master on Wednesday, I do not propose to take them away from you.

Representing Katharine, Sir Charles Russell agreed to a settlement. Of the £144,000 (£9,072,000) estate, Katharine and Willie and their children were given half, while the other litigants divided the balance. Katharine and Willie received a life interest on £25,000 (£1,575,000) each, with an immediate cash payment of £6,000 (£378,000) to her and £3,000 (£189,000) to him. On their deaths, the invested money would be divided between the children, with a considerably smaller proportion for Clare and Katie.

Some years later, Katharine lost much of her money through the malfeasance of an embezzler. The balance was invested in a railway company in Canada whose dividends ceased before the First World War. Willie fared better financially, retired to Brighton and died there, aged sixty-five, in 1905.

Over the years, the attitude of the Catholic Church towards Parnell mellowed. His bust, banished from his residence by Archbishop Thomas Croke, was, according to an article in the *Irish Times* of 30 March 1991:

> ... restored to the house by the second last archbishop, Dr. Thomas Morris. It enjoys a dignified setting in the house now occupied by Archbishop Dermot Clifford.

At that date, it was proposed that the bust should instead be displayed in Leinster House, to acknowledge Parnell's contribution to the political life of Ireland.

It is fascinating to visit the places connected with the Parnell/O'Shea story. Charing Cross no longer remains just a railway station, but is where Willie threw out Parnell's portmanteau; and in the fine roof spans of Brighton Railway Station can still be seen the inspiration for a farm building at Avondale.

On Brighton seafront, the house in Walsingham Terrace where Parnell died has been demolished, but 39 Bedford Square, where Katharine stayed in 1883 and Parnell visited her, still survives. The exterior has not been changed, but the interior has recently been incorporated into the Brighton Hotel, which it adjoins. The old sitting room is now a banqueting area.

Nearby Hove joins Brighton, and 8 Medina Terrace is not far away from Bedford Square. By comparison with old photographs, it can be seen that the house has been slightly extended, on the ground, first and second floors, to the depth of the second floor balcony, undoubtedly to enhance the view of the sea. There is no fire escape (as Willie said) and the rope ladder, suggested in the divorce case, would surely never have been used by Parnell to evade Willie as, apart from the height of the balcony, three sides of the house are plainly visible to any passer-by, and the fourth is joined to 7 Medina Terrace. The house is still known to some locals as 'the place where it all happened'.

The elegant residence at 34 York Terrace, which overlooks Regent's Park, keeps its secrets. A sign declares that the terrace is 'private property' for 'residents only'. It runs behind the present day Planetarium.

Aunt Ben's Eltham Lodge at Court Road, now the club house for the Royal Blackheath Golf Club, is in splendid condition with its original staircase and paintings. Stepping into the hall brings to mind Aunt Ben's rule:

> ... no one should tread upon the highly polished floors, and, as the two large halls had only rugs laid about on the shining surface, one had either to make 'tacks' to reach the desired door or seat, or take a short cut on tiptoe and risk her 'displeasure'....

The billiard room tapestry, hidden in her time, has been uncovered. A door in a lovely bright corner of the first floor leads to, 'The O'Shea Room'. It is where Katharine slept while visiting.

Wonersh Lodge, which stood on the northern side of North Park, was later renamed 'Dunclutha' but, in more recent times, was demolished and replaced by a block of flats. North Park runs at right angles to Court Road and is a continuation (through Court Yard and Tilt Yard) of King John's Walk, which runs past Eltham Palace.

Contrary to Parnell's wishes, Avondale went to his brother, John, who, finding it in debt, sold off many of the trees. In her bedroom in the house, some seven years after Parnell's death, his mother's clothes caught fire, and she died, aged eighty-two. In time, the house was sold to a butcher, who, in turn, sold it to the Irish State. Nowadays, the house contains many items of interest from Parnell's life, and the grounds are beautifully landscaped by the Irish Forestry Commission.

Of Katharine's children, Gerard fought in the First World War. In 1936 he objected to the portrayal of his father in Schauffler's play on Parnell and later became an adviser to a Hollywood film on the same subject, after which all trace of him seems lost. Carmen married a doctor, Arthur Herbert Buck, by whom she had three children. She was divorced because of her adultery with Edward Lucas, who married her and later inherited a baronetcy. It was said that she became an alcoholic. She died in 1921. Clare married an Irish doctor, Bertram Maunsell, and sadly died in 1911, giving birth to a son. This boy, called Assheton Clare Bowyer-Lane Maunsell, had a great likeness to Parnell. His head, according to Norah, was 'just the shape of his grandfather's'. He became an officer in the British Army, serving in India, but died, alas, of enteric fever in 1934, and was buried at Lahore. Katie, too, showed a preference for the British Army by marrying a Captain Louis D'Oyley Horsford Moule. They had one still-born child. In later life she lived in reduced circumstances, and ended her days, as had some of her ancestors, with mental trouble, dying in 1947.

Norah, who outlived her mother by just two years and is buried beside her in Littlehampton, devoted her life entirely to her. Katharine had moved from one rented house to another in Parnell's time, and continued to do so afterwards. On 1 February 1921, just before her mother's death, Norah wrote to Henry Harrison:

> On the strength of your having been such a 'stand-by' and help
> to my dear mother ... when Parnell died ... I am writing to tell
> you that your old friend is dying, slowly and painfully, of heart
> disease. She was seventy-six last Sunday, and has been very ill
> for some months. Now, the doctors say, it is only a question of
> how long she can keep up the fight against death ... She has
> the happy delusion that Parnell comes to her at night, when
> things are worst, and draws her 'out of the black waves'... She
> has never stopped mourning Parnell and I, knowing the misery
> of her heart and soul, have spent my life in keeping her from
> the follies of so many human ways of 'forgetting for a little
> while' when I could; and when I couldn't in nursing her back
> to health and sanity. Her periods of delusion have always been
> Parnell, Parnell, Parnell.

In 1936, Winston Churchill wrote of Parnell:

> We see the man, one of the strangest, most baffling person-
> alities that ever trod the world's stage. He never forgot. He
> never forgave. He never faltered. He dedicated himself to a
> single goal, the goal of Ireland a nation, and he pursued it
> unswervingly until a rose thrown across his path opened a new
> world, the world of love. And, as he had previously sacrificed
> all for Ireland, so, when the moment of choice came, he sacri-
> ficed all, even Ireland, for love. A lesser man might have given
> more sparingly and kept more.

# Bibliography

Cohane, J. P., *The Indestructible Irish*, Meredith Press, New York, 1969.

Craig, Maurice & the Knight of Glin, *Ireland Observed*, The Mercier Press, Cork, 1970.

Ervine, St. John, *Parnell*, Ernest Benn, London, 1928.

Harrison, Henry, *Parnell Vindicated*, Constable & Co., London, 1931.

Horgan, John J., *Parnell to Pearse*, Browne & Nolan, The Riverview Press, Dublin, 1949.

Lanigan, K.M. and Tyler, G., *Kilkenny, Its Architecture and History*, Appletree Press, Belfast, 1977.

Lyons, F.S.L., *Charles Stewart Parnell*, Collins, London, 1977.

Lyons, F.S.L., *The Fall of Parnell 1890-91*, Routledge & Kegan Paul, London, 1960.

MacBride, Maud Gonne, *A Servant of the Queen*, Victor Gollancz, London, 1974.

Morley, John, *The Life of William Ewart Gladstone*, (Vol. II), Macmillan & Company, London, 1912.

O'Brien, C. Cruise, *Parnell & his Party — 1880-90*, Clarendon Press, Oxford, 1968.

O'Brien, R. Barry, *The Life of Charles Stewart Parnell*, (Vol. II), Smith Elder & Company, London, 1899.

O'Brien, W., *The Parnell of Real Life*, T. Fisher Unwin, London, 1926.

O'Connor, T.P., *The Parnell Movement*, Kegan Paul, Trench & Co., London, 1886.

O'Shea, Katharine, *Charles Stewart Parnell*, Cassell, London, 1973.

Shute, Nerina, *More London Villages*, Robert Hall, London,1981.

Yeats, W.B., *Selected Poetry*, edited by A.N. Jeffares, Pan Books, Macmillan, London, 1978.

## JOURNALS AND NEWSPAPERS

*Belfast Evening Telegraph*, 8 Dec. 1890.
*Daily Telegraph*, 17 Nov. 1890.
Dublin *Daily Express*, 2 Nov. 1888.
*Freeman's Journal*, 30 Dec. 1889, 18 Nov. 1890, 1 Dec. 1890, 5 Dec. 1890.
*Irish Medical Times*, 25 Jan. 1991.
*Irish Times*, 17 Nov. 1890, 5 Nov. 1891, 30 March 1991.
*Labour World*, 20 Nov. 1890.
*Observatory, The*, November 1891 (Letter from W.F. Denning,

Bristol).
*Pall Mall Gazette*, 24 May 1886.
*Sussex Daily News*, Oct. 1886.
*Times, The*, 7 March 1887, 18 April 1887.
*United Ireland*, 23 Oct. 1886, 13 Dec. 1890.

# THE LOVE STORY OF YEATS AND MAUD GONNE

## Margery Brady

A dramatic and compelling story of the great love of W. B. Yeats for the woman he immortalised in his poems.

# THE RED-HAIRED WOMAN
## and other Irish Stories

## Sigerson Clifford

'This collection of stories has humour, shrewd observation, sharp wit at times, and the calm, sure touch of the accomplished storyteller ...' *Brendan Kennelly*

# THE WALK OF A QUEEN

## Annie M. P. Smithson

A fascinating story of passion and intrigue set against the backdrop of the War of Independence.

# WHERE WE SPORTED AND PLAYED

## Teddy Delaney

A poignant and atmospheric portrayal of a child's life in Cork City in the early 1950s and 1960s.